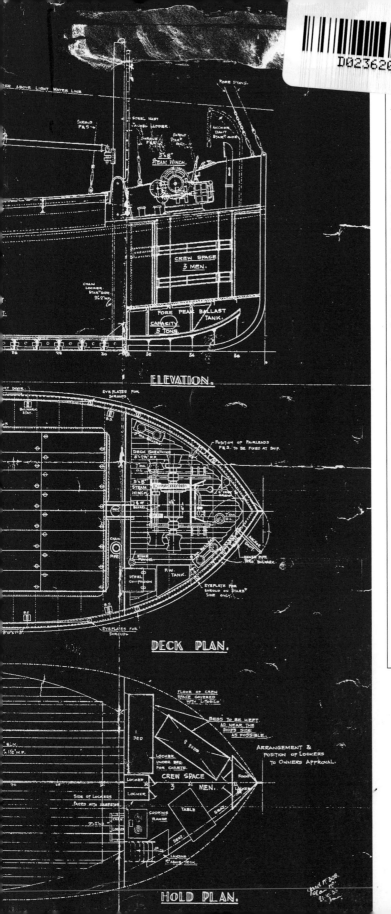

...duction of what ... & Marshall ...*ght*.

Although built as late as 1935, by Ferguson Brothers of Port Glasgow, with her 66 foot length and 18 foot beam, she was a typical Forth & Clyde Canal boat and had she been built fifty years earlier the drawing would have been little different. All the early puffers conformed to this basic design irrespective of owner or builder.

With her crew of three, to whom fifteen feet of the hull length was given for their accommodation, she would only have traded in the Canal and the upper reaches of the Clyde Estuary. Her thirty-four foot hold and her hatch coamings provided 5,500 cubic feet of space, enough for a cargo of approximately 110 tons of coal. The helmsman was exposed to the weather and steering was accomplished by a wheel via chain to a tiller.

ELEVATION.

DECK PLAN.

HOLD PLAN.

THE LIGHT IN THE GLENS

The Rise and Fall of the Puffer Trade

Hays' *Serb* discharging on the beach at Islay.

THE
Light
IN THE
Glens

The Rise and Fall of the Puffer Trade

LEN PATERSON

By the same author
Twelve Hundred Miles for Thirty Shillings
Only Thirty Birthdays

ISBN 0-948905-78-6

Typeset by Posthouse Printing & Publishing,
Findhorn, Forres
Printed in Great Britain
by Redwood Books, Trowbridge
for House of Lochar
Colonsay, Argyll

CONTENTS

ACKNOWLEDGEMENTS 7

MAP 8

1 PROLOGUE 9
    Introduction to the story of the puffers and Glenlight Shipping

2 THE RISE
    Birth Pangs
    The technological advances in the 1850s that led to
    the evolution of the puffer 11
    Locks' Law
    The influence of the Crinan and Forth & Clyde canals on the
    design of the puffers 14
    From Steam to Hydraulics
    The technical development of the puffer from 1856 to the 1990s 20
    The Hays and the Hamiltons
    The rise and growth of three famous puffer firms which came together
    in the 1960s 37
    Ross and Marshall
    The development of this Greenock company from the 1840s until
    the formation of Glenlight 48

3 THE TRADE
    Beaches and Ports
    How the puffers serviced the West Highlands 58
    Real 'Para Handy' Tales
    Collection of real happenings of the kind that the puffermen
    might have told Neil Munro 65
    Of Coal, Whisky and Seaweed
    The economics of the puffer business after the Second World War 71

4 THE FALL

The Light in the Glens
  The formation of Glenlight Shipping Ltd   79
The Vital Subsidy
  Glenlight's trading problems in the 1970/80s   89
The Seven Year War
  The long battle with Government over subsidies   96
The Light Extinguished
  The withdrawal of Government support and Glenlight's closure   101

5 EPILOGUE

109
  The future for West Highlands sea transport

APPENDICES

    I Lighter Owners   111
   II Lighter Builders   113
  III J. Hay and Sons Ltd., operating results 1938   114
   IV Ross and Marshall Ltd., profit/loss account for 1882   115
    V Ross and Marshall Ltd., profit/loss account for SS *Daylight*, 1879   115
   VI Ships' Logs 1880–1963   116
  VII Stowage Measurements   118
 VIII Lighter Ownership 1939–1966   120
   IX Company Liveries   121
    X Why T.R.S. Did and Did Not Work   122
   XI Effect of Government Subsidy in H.I.D.B. Area Trading, 1979–1987   123
  XII Commodities Carried Annually by Glenlight Shipping Ltd., 1973–1993   124
 XIII Tonnages Delivered to Highlands in 1987 by Glenlight Shipping Ltd.   125
  XIV Development of the Tug and Barge Concept for the Shipment of Timber   126

INDEX OF SHIPS

128

ACKNOWLEDGEMENTS

My thanks are due to many people who helped with the production of this book. My former colleagues, Angela Hemphill, who turned my hieroglyphics into a readable typescript, and Alex Fawcett, the last Managing Director of Glenlight Shipping, who read and commented on the draft, are due particular thanks. Gerry Banks, Roy Marshall and Tom Dunn of Clyde Consultants, all shipping men of the Clyde, provided technical advice and practical assistance.

In researching material on the Hay companies, Mrs Isobel Hay was most helpful in giving me access to family papers in her possession and Don Martin of the William Patrick Library, Kirkintilloch, guided me through its documentary and pictorial archive.

Also of great help in researching and sourcing photographic material were Dr W. Lind of the Ballast Trust, Deborah Haase and Susie Stirling at the Museum of Transport, Kelvin Hall, Glasgow, Vanora Skelley at the Glasgow University Business Archive, and Jim Tidesley, Veronica Hartwich and Jim Grant of the Scottish Maritime Museum, Irvine.

Finally tribute is due to Georgina Hobhouse, who acted as editor to the book, whose painstaking and tactful devil's advocacy clarified many of the obscurities in the text that my style of expression had introduced. (She would have hated the construction of this last sentence.) The reader owes her much.

Photographs

As far as has been possible I have tried to give credit to the source of the photographs used in this book. But, particularly on a subject of such public popularity as the puffers, it has proved very difficult to identify original sources. I was surprised, several times, to find that, pictures given to me by former colleagues in good faith as their own, or that I had found or bought and considered to be my property, turned up, not just in one, but several catalogued collections. Perhaps the puffer belongs to everybody. In any case I apologise hereby to anyone who reads this book and sees his or her picture and is not given a proper acknowledgement.

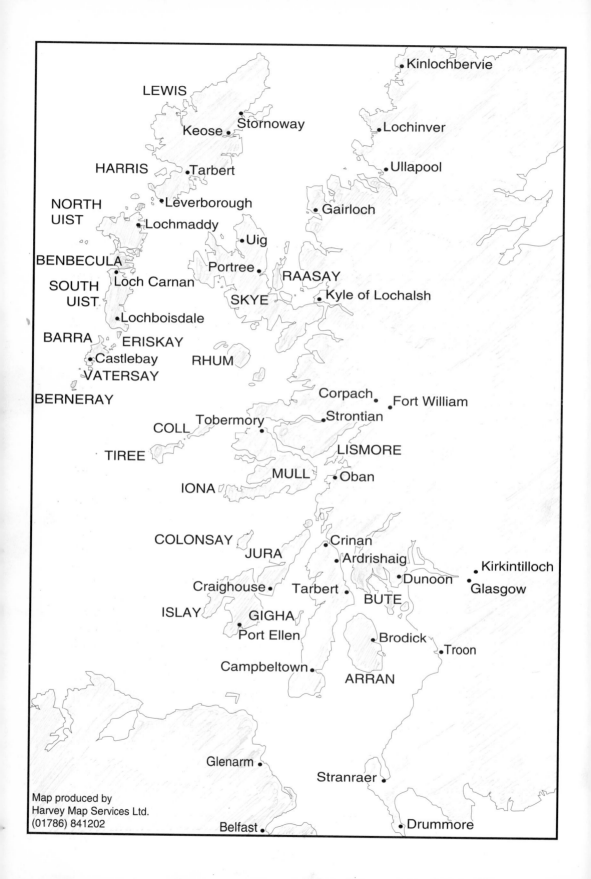

Map produced by
Harvey Map Services Ltd.
(01786) 841202

1

PROLOGUE

When, in December 1993, Glenlight Shipping decided it could no longer take cargoes northwards to the West Highlands and Islands the puffer trade really died. Glenlight was the last shipping company to devote the greater part of its resources and time to the servicing of Scotland's remote Western communities. Many factors conspired to make this withdrawal inevitable. These will be dealt with later. Glenlight's going was not unmourned or unsung but neither was it prevented. And yet it might have been, as those who have the stamina to stay till the closing chapters can judge for themselves. Now that the dust has settled a little it is possible, just, to look back with some objectivity and put Glenlight in its historical context.

Though some disputed it at the time, Glenlight Shipping did truly qualify as the last of the puffer companies. Through its parents, the Hamiltons, the Hays and Ross and Marshall, it could trace its history back to the 1850s. These companies were long term and significant players in the trade. No disrespect is intended in this claim to H. Carmichael who owned two ships at one time and retired in 1984 or to Easdale Shipping who came on to the scene in the 1980s and outlasted Glenlight by a few months. To tell the Glenlight story through that of its antecedents to its own demise in 1993 is genuinely to give a history of the puffer trade.

One other qualification must be made.

It was essential in the West Highland trade to be able to self load and self discharge cargo. Many ships and companies operated on the Western seaboard and took goods and passengers to remote locations. We must be strict and insist that if they did not have cargo gear then they must be disqualified from inclusion in the definition. In any case such ships almost certainly would not have developed from the same roots, the canal boats, as the genuine article. Above all they were unlikely to have the simple engines that exhausted their steam directly into the atmosphere. In other words they did not puff.

How many puffers were there? It has been claimed that four hundred were built for the canal and coastal trades, both east and west. A list of three hundred names was compiled simply in the process of researching this book. For some names only a tattered snapshot is evidence of existence. For others full details of date of launch, builder, owner, technical specification and much else besides has survived. The list contains only a few of the 'Alphabetical' series of names of the Leith, Hull and Hamburg Steam Packet Company lighters. But it may be safe to presume that they owned more than twenty since the evidence includes records of '*A*' and '*Z*'. Similarly, the romantic system that the Carron Company had of giving their craft numbers instead of names allows us to assume that if there was a 'No. 10' in 1871 and a 'No. 12' in 1878, there might well have been a 'No. 11' somewhere in between. In this catalogue are all those vessels of modern vintage that continued to serve the West Highlands until the demise of Glenlight Shipping in 1993. The purist would not consider these to be puffers but they kept the business alive and are worthy of inclusion. It is not difficult therefore to extend the numbers beyond the three hundred mark if not actually all the way to the next hundred. But as the trade lasted for one hundred and forty years we could easily settle for four hundred. They were all clones. Until 1953 they were either 66 or 88 feet long with little variation in beam, draft or engine power.

It was unusual for the term 'puffer' to be used by those who worked in the trade. 'The boats', 'the ships' or 'the wee boats' were terms in frequent use when skippers, crew and office staff discussed operations. Only when talking to outsiders did the word 'puffer' come into play as a shorthand way of conveying to the general public what business they were engaged upon. Jock Thampson and all his bairns were familiar with the puffer from the writings of Neil Munro and their various broadcast adaptations and derivatives. In truth, a pufferman did not really care to be associated with the Para Handy image

which did not do justice to the serious commercial business that he was engaged upon or to the hardworking and often dangerous life that the crews lived. If the term gave a convenient description to the outsider, so be it. To the many fine practical seamen in the trade the jokey devil-may-care reputation of the crew of the 'Vital Spark' was far removed from the reality of life. There were of course rogues, vagabonds, saints and sinners, humour and tragedy afloat and ashore. But you find that in all walks of life. Out of deference to erstwhile colleagues ashore and afloat the term 'puffer' is used sparingly throughout this book.

Before tracing the commercial history of the two main groups of companies that came together to form Glenlight Shipping some space has been devoted to outlining the technical development of the unique vessel that evolved to become the maritime workhorse of Scotland's Western Seaboard. The puffer kept on developing from the 1850s to the 1990s and it seemed logical to tell this story early in the book and then to retrace our steps and examine the start-up and progress of Ross and Marshall and Hay-Hamilton.

The Light in the Glens intends to set down the story of Glenlight Shipping, to put it in its social and economic context and to pay tribute, however inadequately, to those who worked in the puffer trade.

2

THE RISE

Birth Pangs

The self-propelled barge, steam lighter or puffer did not come from a blinding flash of inspiration. There was no Archimedean 'Eureka' announcing its conception. It was a child of Scotland's industrial revolution, a product of that peculiarly fertile technological enlightenment of the West of Scotland in the early nineteenth century. Like much else in that period its parents were engineering and metallurgy. Its antecedents were not to be found in any breeder's form book (it may even have been born out of wedlock) but like most mongrels, it proved to be up to the tasks set for it, and then some.

As a shareholder of the Forth & Clyde Canal Company, lying in your bath in the late 1840s, you might well have cried out 'Eureka' when you realised that all you had to do was put together an iron hull, a steam engine and a propeller to solve the problem of competing with those trouble-

The *Charlotte Dundas*, the first successful steam driven ship on the Forth & Clyde Canal. It was feared that wash from her paddles would erode the canal banks. (William Simpson Library, Kirkintilloch)

some newcomers the railways for speed and cost effectiveness.

How would you have put the pieces of this particular jigsaw together? Simply by being aware of all the latest marine technological advances.

Steam power had been established as an industrial force since Mr. Newcomen had introduced his engine to coal mining in 1712. Every Scot took pride in Watt's improvement, patented in 1769, of Newcomen's engine. (He condensed the steam outside the cylinder and thereby freed the engine from the limitations of atmospheric pressure.) It would be unpatriotic to level the accusation that Watt's patent had stultified developments in engines for many years and it may be that Symington, Miller and Taylor in their experiment on Dalswinton Loch, near Dumfries, in 1788, actually infringed on Watt's patent in their engine design. At least they were intent on making progress. Steam driven, their unnamed 25 foot long boat with two centre line paddles within its eight foot beam of twin hulls achieved a speed of 5 m.p.h. (Even this wasn't an original idea but the Marquis D'Abbans' successful steamer, *Pyroscaphe* of 1783, disappeared in the turmoil of the French Revolution.) No commercial development in Scotland followed from this, although Symington re-emerged later as the engine designer for the *Charlotte Dundas*.

The Forth & Clyde Canal Company was determined to experiment with steam power and brought the best experience of the day to the design of the *Charlotte Dundas*. She was a stern wheel paddle ship and successfully towed two barges the eighteen miles from Castlecary to Port Dundas in 1803. She was considered a technical success but judged not to be a commercial one and the experiment was abandoned. As a result, Scotland was to wait nearly a decade for its first commercial steamship in the form of the *Comet*.

Following the *Comet*, the steam paddle ship was to become a well established economic form of commercial shipping, the history of which is well documented. But further technological advance was necessary particularly in the size and power of the marine steam engine to make them suitable for the steam lighter. And of course those protruding paddles took up too much room in canal locks!

The supremacy of the paddle came under threat in 1836 when F.P. Smith patented his screw propeller. A dramatic demonstration of the superiority of the propeller took place in 1845 in the famous tug-of-war between *Alecto* and *Rattler*. During a trial organised by the Royal Navy the screw driven *Rattler* succeeded in towing the paddler *Alecto* backwards at 2.5 m.p.h. As ever, the Royal Navy had conservatively ignored Petit Smith's demonstration of the screw when his 100 foot long *Archimedes* circumnavigated the United Kingdom nearly twenty years earlier. When, also in 1845, ss *Great Britain* became the first British screw steamship to cross the Atlantic all doubts about the propeller were resolved in the minds of many.

The screw was the last piece of the jigsaw to be put in place because iron hulls had been in use for a long time. Locally the *Vulcan*, built in the Monkland Canal in 1819, was the first successful example of constructing a commercial hull in what was a 'new' material for marine use. (A replica of her 61' × 11' × 4' 5" hull can be seen at Summerlee, Coatbridge.) As far back as 1787 Wilkinson had built an iron barge (70' × 6' 5" × 4') for use on the canal at Coalbrookdale, appropriately called *Trial*. So the idea was not entirely novel. In 1822 an iron hulled paddle steamer, the *Aaron Manby*, made a cross channel passage and in 1834 Tod and McGregor built their first iron ship on the Clyde. By 1853 they had stopped wooden construction altogether.

Apart from its superior strength to weight ratio, allowing the construction of larger ships, iron offered the additional virtue of rigidity in a hull. Wooden hulls flexed too much in a sea-way for the critical alignment of engine through propeller shaft to screw to be achieved. The stiffer iron hull gave the confidence that if engine, shaft and propeller were set down in a straight line in the yard then they would stay that way when the vessel took to the water to earn her living.

So the time had arrived that the marine industry had been anticipating for centuries. The pinnacle of marine science and technology was about to be reached. The puffer was about to be created.

In 1856, the Forth & Clyde Canal Company decided to install a twin cylinder steam engine and a propeller in

Vulcan was the first iron hulled vessel built in Scotland. This reconstruction of her was made by the Summerlee Heritage Park for the 1990 Glasgow Garden Festival. Original drawings were used to reproduce faithfully her hull form and layout. Throughout her 50 year working life, carrying passengers on the canals she was horse drawn. The chimney was not for the exhaust of steam from an engine but for the smoke from the stove that provided heat and refreshments for the passengers. (*Photo by Summerlee Heritage Park* where *Vulcan* is now on display)

one of their existing iron-hulled scows (see page 14). She was the *Thomas*. She was successful. She goes down in history as one of mankind's supreme marine achievements! She yields only to a vessel specially built a year later by Swans at Hamiltonhill as being the first new built steam lighter. She was called the *Glasgow*. For one hundred and forty years her successors would build a legend.

Locks' Law

The shipping industry is used to describing its ships in terms of the canals they use. Thus a 'panamax' is a ship that can, just, pass through the locks of the Panama Canal and trade to and from the Pacific without the tedious costly passage round the Horn.

Both the Crinan and Forth & Clyde Canals, equally famously, gave birth to a ship of a specific size. We don't know them as 'crinamax' however, but simply as puffers. One wag coined the phrase 'West

Highland Bulk Carrier' to slyly imply that in their way and in their day these canals and the ships that they spawned held equal economic importance on a world scale to their owners, crews and customers. In the world of shipping mnemonics 'W.H.B.C.' did not have the currency of O.B.O. (oil/bulk/ore) or LASH (lighter aboard ship) but the point was made.

Put at its most basic the locks on the Forth & Clyde were 60 feet long and 20 feet wide. Those of the Crinan were 88 feet long and also 20 feet wide. If you wished to sail across Scotland rather than

Below An extract from the transactions of the Institute of Engineers in Scotland for 1857/8. Mr Neil Robson gave a paper entitled 'On the Navigation of Canals by Screw Steamers' in which he described the conversion of the *Thomas* and presented illustrations. This diagram of the lay-out of the engine, boiler and screw, was one of these. He reported that the screw of four feet pitch, at 130 revolutions per minute, gave a speed of five miles per hour. A pressure of 35 pounds per square inch, in the cylinders, was 'sufficient for propelling the lighter with a full cargo of 70 to 80 tons.'

Opposite above The lighterman's life was not all one of battling westerly gales and tales were told of how fresh milk was surreptitiously obtained when traversing the Crinan Canal. (D. MacDonald Collection)

Opposite below An unknown puffer at the seaward end of the Crinan Canal. She is certainly a very old type and has had wooden bulwarks added to her metal hull. This would have allowed her to trade outside the canal. Also seen is *Linnet* which carried passengers along the Canal to link with steamers for Fort William. Passengers seem to be boarding such a vessel on the outside berth.

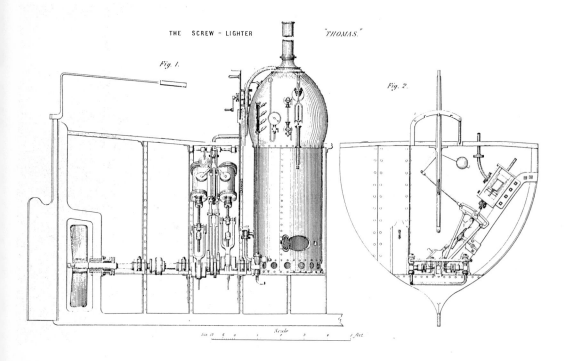

THE SCREW – LIGHTER   *THOMAS.*

Fig. 1.

Fig. 2.

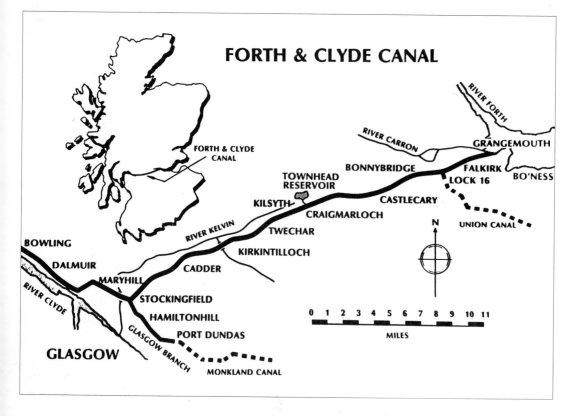

FORTH & CLYDE CANAL

pass the Pentland Firth, sixty-odd feet was the limit put on the overall length of your ship. To take advantage of the nine mile journey from Ardrishaig to Crinan rather than fight tide and weather for 150 miles to round the Mull of Kintyre then your vessel had to be under 90 feet length overall.

Both canals put a similar draught restriction on vessel design of around 9 feet although this was not always achievable in the Crinan where water shortage was for many years a problem. When planned, water depths of between 12 and 15 feet were debated, but in the event the canal opened in 1801 in a semi-finished state with a water depth of only 8 feet. (On two occasions, 1884 and 1890, the Crinan closed due to droughts – in the West of Scotland!) As late as 1958, when the future of the canal was the subject of a special enquiry, commercial vessel owners pleaded for a guaranteed water depth of 10 feet. Only marginally profitable in the first century of its existence it operated at a loss continuously after the First World War. As coasters grew in size, from economic necessity after World War II, they ceased to use the Crinan altogether. By 1965 the number of commercial ships (excluding fishing vessels) passing the waterway had fallen to a fifth of the 1950 level.

By 1962 the Forth & Clyde had closed to all commercial traffic but, of the two canals, it will be remembered for having played the more significant role in the development of the West Highland Bulk Carrier. Construction of the canal started in 1768 and it was officially opened in 1790. It had progressively come into operation as sections became available. Kirkintilloch, which was to become the home of two famous shipyards, was reached by 1773 and ships were recorded as arriving from Bo'ness on the Forth with cargoes of up to 50 tons. By 1777 Hamiltonhill, the other significant boat-building location on the canal, was open to traffic from the East.

The year before the Forth & Clyde opened, Miller, Symington and Taylor had already conducted their steamboat experiment at Dalswinton but it was not until the year of the completion of the Crinan, 1803, that steam propulsion was tried out on the Forth & Clyde. The *Charlotte Dundas*, so called after the daughter of a major shareholder in the canal company, a stern paddle driven steamer, successfully towed two laden 70 ton barges from Lock 20 (Castlecary) to Port Dundas. This eighteen mile stretch, devoid of locks, took just over six hours. While considered a great technical success, the fears for the erosion of the canal banks from her wash caused the experiment to be abandoned. There was also opposition from those with an invest-ment in the alternative and original type of horsepower. To be fair, there was a real problem at the locks where barges could only be taken through in the traditional way and the advantage of steam was largely negated. So eleven years before Harry Bell's *Comet* made its appearance on the Clyde, Scotland's first commercial steamer was set aside through the not unusual reaction to innovation – fear, prej-udice and vested interest.

A sister waterway of the Forth & Clyde, the Monkland Canal, linked in 1791, saw the birth, in 1819, of the first Scottish vessel ever built in malleable iron. From that time on, builders of the canal scows and barges began to use this product of the nearby Iron Burgh of Coatbridge in their constructions. It was not until the late 1830s that iron shipbuilding began on the Clyde in earnest. *Vulcan* was commis-sioned by the Forth & Clyde Canal Company and was horse-drawn

throughout her passenger and cargo carrying life.

Steam was introduced to the Forth & Clyde again in 1828 to combat the growing threat of the railways (presumably market forces overcame objections to the wash created) in the form of the paddler *Cupid*. She carried passengers at an oper-ating speed of 3 knots. It is not clear if she towed barges but there would have been no technical reason why she could not.

Commercial steam had come earlier to the Crinan in 1819 when Bell's *Comet* used it to make voyages from Glasgow to Fort William with passengers, but these paddle ships never really developed into efficient carriers of bulk cargoes because so much of the vessel's beam, limited by the size of the locks, had to be given over to paddle boxes. (There was little room left for barges in the Forth & Clyde locks when

The 1923 *Pibroch* passes the 1944 *Smeaton* in the Crinan Canal. *Smeaton*, owned by Warnock Bros. of Paisley, but built as VIC 33 at Northwich, is light-ship while *Pibroch* is clearly lower in the water. She has barrels on deck, (surely not whisky?) and two of her crew are taking time off from stowing the bunker coal to exchange news with a tea-drinking friend on *Smeaton*.

the 56 foot long and 18 foot beam *Charlotte Dundas* was in.) The puffer truly evolved from the self-propelled barge or lighter rather than these paddle ships. Even the Clyde's luggage boats which traded from Port Glasgow to Glasgow itself before they succumbed to the railways and other changes were a different breed.

The Forth & Clyde Canal Company met the challenge of the railways in two interesting ways. In 1833 barges were constructed that took railway wagons straight off the tracks of the Monkland and Kirkintilloch Railway to take coal to Glasgow and beyond. The Forth & Clyde invented the first Ro-Ro ferry? In an attempt to make canal transport match the speed of the burgeoning railways a steam locomotive was introduced to pull a train of nine vessels from Lock 16 (Falkirk) westwards.

A speed of nearly 20 knots was achieved pulling single ships and while the towed train of two laden scows and seven sea-going schooners was constrained to the allowed limit of 3½ m.p.h. it was judged that greater speed was possible. The logic pointed to building a light railway the length of the canal to tow barges. But if that was done why was a canal needed? The concept was not developed. The only solution in the long term was to power the barges themselves.

Opposite above and below Princess Mayse was built as late as 1893 but gives an example of what the gabbert, those forerunners of the puffers, looked like. With an overall length of 54 feet, a beam of 17 and a draft of 6 she could use the Forth & Clyde Canal and could have sailed out to the West coast. She traded until after World War II and these photographs probably date from this period. She has had an auxiliary engine fitted, (the stern view shows her propeller) and this together with a block fitted to the end of her gaff provided mechanical assistance for the discharge of cargo. The greater reliability of the steam driven lighter based on its independence from wind power gradually pushed the gabberts from the seas.

Like the Crinan, the Forth & Clyde traffic was entirely powered by sail and horse. Sea-going sloops to a draft of 8 feet and a length of 60 feet could carry cargo of 70 to 90 tons and in this fashion grain, iron ore and coal moved along the canal in both directions to the termini and to west and east coast Scottish ports beyond them. The dumb barges moved these commodities to destinations within the canal system which included the Monkland, Union and Forth & Clyde Canals. This was the trade that needed to be mechanised if the competition of the railways was to be met.

And so it was to be. In 1856 a boiler and engine, costing £320, and a shaft and propeller were fitted to the Canal Company's lighter *Thomas* and the first puffer was born. A speed of up to 5 knots was possible and was allowed. The economics of barging were transformed. The *Thomas* had a crew of two. As a scow she had needed two boatmen, a horse and a horseman. By 1860 there were 25 steamers on the Forth & Clyde and by 1866 there were 70. The day of the horse-drawn barge was not quite over but eventually they and the schooners and gabberts were to lose out to steam as the self-propelled barges went beyond the confines of the canals to carry cargo to the East and particularly the West Coast of Scotland. The Forth & Clyde was to have nearly another hundred years of useful life. At its peak, in the year of 1913, almost seven hundred thousand tons of cargo passed through it. It suffered a loss of traffic during the First World War but its real decline commenced in the 1930s. During all of this period the canals dictated the size of the lighters/ships. The law of the locks applied throughout.

It was not until 1963, when the diesel engined *Glensheil* came into service in the West Highland trade, that a vessel was built that could use neither of the two canals.

From Steam to Hydraulics

Once the breakthrough with steam propulsion of lighters had been made on the Forth & Clyde with *Thomas* and *Glasgow* in 1857, it was logical to consider how to expand their range so that trade could be conducted outwith the confines of the canal. After all, the canal was only a transit for many of the sailing ships that used it and their loading ports and destinations were far from Grangemouth and Bowling. There were many technical problems to be solved before the mechanised lighter could compete with the schooners and gabberts.

The hull form of the scow had evolved to suit the conditions in the canal. It had no bulwarks as they would have interfered in the loading and discharging of cargo. Hatch coamings and covers were not considered necessary; even in high winds waves were unlikely to break over the bow and swamp the vessel in the canal. Masts and derricks were unknown because cargo working was available from shoreside facilities. Simple tillers were all that were necessary for steering. The rudder forces involved in keeping a scow on the straight and narrow, in the placid canal at the leisurely pace of a horse, were well within the capabilities of a reasonably robust man. (Steering wheels did not arrive until the 1870s and even then were not universally fitted.) The first simple puffing engines were inefficient in their use of fresh water as they blew it up their lums, directly exhausting steam to atmosphere. The canal provided a plentiful supply of this essential commodity but it was definitely scarce beyond the sea-locks. Eventually the classic West Coast puffer was to evolve as technology advanced and, in time, three different forms of steam lighter emerged for three distinct trades.

Before all this it was important to free the lighter from having to use the canal as its fresh water source. The surface condenser did this. As an 'invention' it had been around since 1836 when Wingate introduced it in conjunction with his steam engines. The canal trade benefited from the advances in design of the 1854 to 1874 period, when Elder patented his compound engine and he and/or Wingate devised the triple expansion engine. This was the engine that was to dominate marine propulsion technology until the 1920s when the internal combustion engine began to replace steam in a significant way.

Certainly by the 1870s compound engines, condensers and steel boilers, which could withstand high pressures better than iron ones, had transformed the range and efficiency of the lighter. In effect puffers stopped puffing from then on. The engine in the *Glasgow* had a 14 inch diameter cylinder and an operating stroke of 14 inches and the whole delivered 20 horsepower to drive her 60 gross tons (a cargo deadweight of around 90 tons). The typical compound engine, which with variations was installed in lighters until World War II, had a 12 inch high pressure cylinder delivering steam to a 20 inch low pressure cylinder thence to the condenser to be returned to the boiler via a feed pump. Input pressure from the 12ft × 6ft diameter boiler was around 100 lbs per square inch. The horsepower was again about 20 but the compound engine's coal consumption was 30% lower than the single cylinder engine. This could be translated into increased steaming range or greater cargo capacity.

It was not difficult to fit bulwarks, hatch coamings and hatch covers to make the lighter more seaworthy. Setting up masts and derricks for cargo handling presented no problem either. It was the steam winch coupled with these last two that gave the steamer a critical advantage over the sailing ship. This mechanical aid made a

Pictured here at Paisley, in 1902, loading a bagged cargo, *Tom Moore* was registered in Glasgow in 1899 but was probably a good deal older. With a draft of 5ft 4ins she could have worked on the Forth & Clyde Canal and the absence of bulwarks confirms that, in concept, she was a canal boat. Unlike *Kelpie* (p23) she was tiller steered. She is reported as being 'rebuilt 1892' and perhaps at that time the mast and derrick were added. (National Maritime Museum)

A rare sight – a lighter under sail. Until about the early 1900s it was customary to fit the 'outside boats' with sails, a practice that stopped as equipment, especially engines, became more reliable. There are many recorded instances of lighters completing their voyages under sail after engine failures. The minutes of J. & J. Hay recorded in 1899 that the *Gael* made a passage under sail from Wemyss Bay to Greenock after her tail shaft broke and her propeller fell off. In this picture does the absence of smoke from the puffer's lum suggest that she had only sail power available? (Scottish Maritime Museum)

world of difference to the speed with which cargo could be discharged apart from being a considerable aid for warping and anchor handling. The gabbert, dependent on wind and tide for arrival and muscle power for discharging, (unless an auxiliary engine was fitted), was at a considerable disadvantage compared to the speed, independence of conditions (relatively) and ease of cargo handling of the steam lighter.

The puffer evolved into three forms depending on the trade engaged in. The canals dominated thinking for many years and a breed of 'inside' boats emerged which were still basically powered canal scows. Their draught was dictated by Forth & Clyde or even Monkland Canal depths. In 1875 Hay, who had been a barge master on the Forth & Clyde since 1857, built *Leopold* at their yard at Kirkintilloch. With her 13 foot beam and 5 foot draft she was narrow enough and shallow enough for the Forth & Clyde. She had a single cylinder 10 HP engine and a deadweight of 50 tons and was intended for Monkland and Forth & Clyde work but made occasional forays outside the canals. Ross and Marshall, the Greenock lighterage company which also dated back to the 1850s, built a similar vessel, *Sunlight*, in 1876. She was slightly larger, with a deadweight of 65 tons and a 20 HP engine and given the company's location was intended for both canal and estuary work. Both were crewed by three men.

This crew complement they shared

with the 'shorehead' boats, the second category, which were estuary vessels first and canal boats second. Their area of operation on the Clyde was limited to what would today be recognised as smooth water limits. The regulatory authorities proscribed their venturing south of a line from Skipness on Kintyre to Garroch Head on Bute. Beyond this demarcation, or 'outside the line', the Board of Trade took an interest in matters like freeboard, hatch covers and fastenings, load lines and the number of crew, usually specifying four. Shorehead boats were therefore usually 66ft long, had a crew of 3 and carried 80 to 90 tons. The 'outside' boats would be 66ft and carried 110/120 tons of cargo for their crew of four to work. Hays' *Briton* (1893) typified this design (65' 8" length, 18' beam, 8' 4" draft with a 17HP engine) and, apart from the fact that she was the last that they built with an iron hull, they did not depart much from the basic design for the next forty years.

For the outside boats they had to experiment to find a seaworthy hull form, as the basic shape of the canal scow was less than ideal for the Minches in winter. It was a process of trial and error with much empiricism and little or no theory. The Hays bought from other builders (Swans at Hamiltonhill in the early days) and learned. They experimented by 'engining' an iron schooner and learned. They learned well; as the adoption of their design, by the Admiralty in 1939, for a whole series of lighters showed. They built by hand and eye and it was not until 1912 that the Hay directors considered asking Scotts of Bowling to make drawings of their latest ship. Go to the Kirkintilloch Library and there you will find today their Yard Manager's notebook setting out the offsets for the hulls of four steamers. Fellows of the Royal Institute of Naval Architects might be surprised but this is all that was necessary to build seaworthy hulls.

Ross and Marshall, though they built for themselves at their riverside premises at Greenock, and like the Hays were too small a yard to maintain a design department, had no need for such rule of thumb methods. Being in the middle of one of the world's great shipbuilding centres and having bought more vessels than they built themselves, their optimum hull design emerged fairly quickly. Their 66ft Forth & Clyde boat was remarkably like that of the Hays. They had an eye more firmly fixed on the West Coast trade and saw the

The *Kelpie* was built in 1868 and is a good example of the very early puffer with her rudimentary boiler and engine casing and open wheel aft of the lum. Her high bulwarks and sails mark her out as an outside boat in contrast to the *Tom Moore*. (p21)

Otter, was built in 1886 and in general appearance is little different from *Kelpie*, although nearly 20 years older. There seems to be evidence of a certain social distinction between the bowler-hatted group of four aft and the cloth-capped group who have just seen to the loading of the bucket, which the winchman, just discernible in the bow, is swinging overside. The location is thought to be Easdale in Argyll, in which case there would almost certainly have been a cargo of slates for the Clyde area.

advantage of separating the design of the shorehead boat from that of the outside boat. Consequently they developed an outside boat that was larger than Hays', being limited in length by the dimensions of the Crinan rather than the Forth & Clyde Canal.

The classic puffer hull, which changed little until after World War II, irrespective of the 88ft or 66ft length, was bluff forward and was by no means flat bottomed as has been assumed by many, from knowledge of their beaching activities. Bilges were rounded and there was a rise of several inches from the strong bar keel (around five inches deep) to allow the

bilges to drain to the centre line. Underwater there was a noticeable upward slope (sheer) of the hull lines both at stem and stern. The quarter deck was raised and would account for between a quarter and a third of the overall length. This provided additional buoyancy to the hull and space for bunkers and machinery. Steering, compass and engine controls were on this deck, sometimes before the lum and sometimes aft of it. The helmsman's protection varied from canvas dodgers to rudimentary wheel houses, the latter being considered a hazard to navigation for many years. Forward of the quarter deck was the hold with coamings and bulwarks according to purpose and beyond that in the foremost area was the crew accommodation. Usually a generous 15 feet was allowed for three or four men although a separate cabin for the master was provided aft, attached to the wheelhouse if one existed. On deck there was a steam winch for cargo working, the mast, which could be lowered, as could the lum on many, for passing the bridges on the upper reaches of the Clyde, and the derrick. The lifting capacity of the derrick was between 1 and 5 tons. Buckets and grabs for carrying cargo made up the essential equipment. Pretty they were not. But they had the inherent attractiveness of a functional creation. As one no-nonsense Clyde marine superintendent said to a new young colleague who was taken aback by the well-used appearance of one working lighter, 'She's no meant to be your Daddy's yacht'. In the author's view it was not until after the Hay-Hamilton amalgamation in the 1960s produced *Glenfyne* and *Glencloy* that aesthetics and functionality were successfully married. These ships, in a sense the last of the puffer tradition, looked and were the part. Like the Spitfire they combined a sense of purpose with good appearance. You looked at them and you knew what they were for. No apology is made for the comparison with Britain's most famous fighting plane.

By increasing the overall length to 88ft Ross and Marshall were able to push their cargo capacity up to 180 tons with significant economic advantage. Mr. Isambard Brunel had demonstrated that while the capacity of a ship varied with the cube of its main dimensions the power required to push it through the water varied only by the square of those same dimensions. Hence the cargo increase to 180 tons was accomplished at the expense of a modest increase from about 20 to 24 horsepower. The *Warlight* (1919) exemplified this

The Stem and Stern of It. This picture of the 1911 *Invercloy*, of G. & G. Hamilton, and the 1910 *Ardfern*, of Dougall and Stirrat, gives a good overall view of the sea-going lighter of the period. The *Invercloy* was built by the Larne Shipbuilding Company and the *Ardfern* by P. McGregor and Co. on the Forth and Clyde Canal. Yet the stern of the latter could be fitted on the forward section of the former quite comfortably. Apart from the solid bulwark aft on the Scottish built boat and the rails on the Irish one there is very little to tell them apart.

concept and was 86' long, with a beam of 18' 6" and a draft of 9' 2". Lighters were not built much bigger than this for another forty years when the Crinan restriction was finally abandoned.

In 1912 all lightermens' eyes were once again focussed on Kirkintilloch, not on Hays' yard, but on that of their next door neighbour, Peter McGregor and Sons Ltd. They were about to break with tradition and launch a lighter with an internal combustion engine. Were all those steamers about to become obsolete overnight? Here was the possibility, because of savings in space and weight in not having to carry a 12 ft boiler full of

water and 11 tons of coal to feed it, of a 66 ft boat being able to carry 30 tons more cargo, 25% more than the conventional lighter.

J.M. Paton, of Paton and Hendry, managers of Glasgow Steam Coasters Ltd, had formed a new company, the Coasting Motor Shipping Company Ltd and ordered six motor driven coasters of canal size from McGregor to explore the possibilities of this new form of marine propulsion. The first to come off the slips was *Innisgara* (65' 6" long, 18' 4" beam and 8' 7" draft) and she had an overhang aft through which the exhaust passed, there being no lum. She and two of her sisters had two-stroke Swedish engines giving 80 BHP. Two others had Dutch engines which generated 110 HP and the sixth, *Innisbeg* had an 80 HP two cylinder engine made by Beardmore of Glasgow. Paton clearly intended to compare his three different engine types but World War I intervened probably making orderly experimentation difficult. The engines got

The *Innisgara*, the first motorised lighter, is seen here as she is about to be launched from McGregor's yard at Kirkintilloch in 1912. (Like Hays' ships, because of the restrictions imposed by the width of the canal, all vessels from McGregor's were launched sideways.) The stem of one of her sister ships can be seen beyond the *Innisgara*'s stern. In all, eight of these motorised vessels were built in 1912/13. (William Simpson Library, Kirkintilloch)

a bad reputation for reliability. The inexperience of the operators may well have been a factor in this. At any rate the fleet had been dispersed by the end of the war and no other owner took up the challenge. No doubt the Hays, with a fleet of twenty two potentially obsolescent steam vessels, breathed a sigh of relief and got on with life.

Sir William Beardmore, who at that time was investing heavily in the Scottish motor vehicle industry and the design of internal combustion engines, was a director of J & J Hay. It is interesting to speculate on why he did not persuade the Hays to take up the motor engine experi-

Sir James was a Knottingley-built VIC, No. 82, and was one of the 'improved' 80 foot versions developed in England during the War. She is clearly different in appearance from the classic Hays design and frankly is not as pleasing to the eye. They had a reputation of being difficult to steer. Nevertheless her 165 dwt offered commercial attractions to Hay who purchased her in 1953. (D. MacDonald Collection)

ment once the *Innisbeg* had broken the ground. It is also interesting to ponder on how different the development of the Scottish coaster would have been had the Hays been persuaded and had they then made a success of the venture. The balance between the economics of sea and road transport would have been quite

```
              Screw Lighter "ANZAC"

              Report on trial trip.

Date      14th Sept. 1939
Condition of ship:-

              Complete

              Cargo      111 Tons coal

              Bunker      12    "

                           6    " coal in bags.


Drafts before leaving Queen's Dock:-

              Forward 8'-6"      mean 9'-1¼"

              Aft      9'-9"

Vessel left Bowling about 3.30 p.m. and proceeded to Gareloch.


      Owners Representative on Board    Mr. Alexander.

      Engineers     "      "    "      Mr. Grant.


Vessel made two runs on Gareloch measured mile and results were
as under:-


      Run (1)   Speed   6.89 Knots )   mean speed 7.22 knots
      Run (2)      "    7.55   "   )

      The engines were running at 168 Revs.

      Steam pressure.   108 lbs.

      Back       "       12 lbs.

      Vacuum             24½ "
```

A simple report issued by Scott & Sons of Bowling, the builders of ss *Anzac*, on her speed trials conducted over the measured mile in the Gareloch. (The Gareloch, a sea loch on the Clyde, is only a few miles from Scott's yard at Bowling.) With a full load of 111 tons of coal she achieved an average speed of just over 7 knots, a good speed from a 66 foot long hull.

different in the period between the two World Wars.

There were few major design changes in the inter-war period. The Hays fixed on their established concepts of shorehead and outside boats, all within the 66ft length restriction of their own building yard. Ross and Marshall continued to squeeze more out of their 88 foot steamer culminating in the 1938 *Sealight* of 180 tons deadweight. The Hamiltons did much the same with their second *Glencloy*, of 1930, which was built at Scotts of Bowling to Crinan limits and was powered

by a Gauldie Gillespie compound engine, a make much favoured by coaster owners in the 1920s and 1930s.

When in 1939 the Admiralty looked for a solution to the problems of providing lighterage for their warships and convoys of merchantmen they chose the Hay 66ft design. Earlier that year Hay had taken, for them, the unusual step of not building new vessels at their own yard. Two new ships, *Anzac* and *Lascar*, were delivered from Scotts of Bowling. Copies of their trial reports exist and that of *Anzac* is reproduced on this page. They were built to use the Forth & Clyde and we can see from the report that they could carry 110/120 tons of cargo at a speed of 7 knots. Nearly one hundred of these craft were commissioned by the Admiralty from English yards on the Humber, in Cheshire, Norfolk and on the Tyne and they saw world-wide service. They were designated Victualling Inshore Craft, abbreviated to VIC, and romantically given numbers as names. Only two were built in Scotland, VIC 18, which was built at Kirkintilloch in 1942, purchased by Hay after the war and named *Spartan* and *Kaffir* (Kirkintilloch, 1944) which was actually a VIC order that was cancelled before completion. The decision was made by the Admiralty to specify steam propulsion for these craft. This was a sensible approach because, unlike oil for diesel engines, coal did not have to be imported and some small burden was removed from the load under which Britain's merchant fleet laboured to keep the country supplied with essential supplies. Only eleven were motor vessels and of these, nine were of the original 66 foot class and two were of the 'improved' 80 foot version of which thirty-five were built.

When these vessels came on to the market at the end of the war they became the backbone of the West Highland trade's re-tonnaging programme. They were

The first diesel powered coaster built for the West Highlands, MV *Glenshira*. She was built by Scott and Sons, Bowling, and here is seen on trials on the Clyde in 1953. Hamilton and McPhail completely re-thought the traditional approach and produced an elegant practical ship that was a real advance in coaster design.

available for around £2,000, about half the price of a new-building, if you could get the materials, and they were no more than eight years old. Curiously, none of the nine diesels that would have fitted the Forth & Clyde locks were brought back to Scotland, but, all told, around twenty of the steamers were. The 'big' companies Hay, Ross and Marshall and Hamilton and McPhail bought half of them but the skipper-owners and smaller concerns also saw the benefits to be had in good second-hand tonnage.

In a sense it is a matter of regret that this happened. Steam as a method of marine propulsion had been in decline since the 1920s and would be virtually dead by the end of the 1950s. Because of these purchases the Scottish coaster trade was thirled to the steam engine in its newer ships. The attraction of familiarity with the technology was obvious but the necessary advance to diesel propulsion was delayed to the trade's long term economic disadvantage.

In 1948 Hamilton converted their *Invercloy* to an oil burning steamer and a little time later Hay did the same with *Tuscan*. While this approach went quite a long way to meeting the labour problem, for it was to become increasingly difficult to find personnel with the experience to tend a boiler and the physical strength and inclination to stoke one, it was at best a temporary compromise within a ship design that gave considerable space and deadweight to carrying water, a boiler and a condenser.

In 1953 Hamilton and McPhail, in their first joint new-building, took the plunge and brought out the first diesel-engined lighter, *Glenshira*. She was built to Crinan limits and achieved 190 tons dead-weight capacity and a speed of eight knots

Diesel meets Steam. The advance in the design of the lighter that came with diesel is illustrated in this photograph. The motor vessel *Glenshira* (1953) passes the steam ship *Kaffir* (built as a VIC in 1944) at Dunardry in the Crinan Canal in 1959. In every respect, speed, reliability, cargo carrying and working and crew accommodation the newer vessel was the superior. *Glenshira* was the last to be built that could use the Crinan. Her descendants were larger and faster and faced the passage round the Mull of Kintyre with equanimity.

with her 270 BHP engine. As the picture opposite shows she was not just a motorised puffer. She looked radically different. Rightly, advantage was taken of the modern propulsion system to re-think her, both externally and internally. The steamer consumed 2.0 to 2.5 tons of coal per day for its seven knots and had a maximum range of about five days on its own bunker capacity. (The customer's coal cargo was, of course, sacrosanct and was never used to replenish the ship.) The diesel achieved its eight knots on less than a ton of fuel oil daily.

Scottish Malt Distillers had been shipowners since 1923 and had used their own *Pibroch* for coal and barley into Islay

and for whisky out. Their second *Pibroch* (1957) was the second diesel lighter on the West Coast following the *Glenshira* example and went a step further by fitting steel hatch covers. This was both a safety and a labour saving investment as there was nothing more boring and back breaking than manhandling wooden hatch covers into position and securing them with a tarpaulin and wooden chocks. It was also suggested at the time that the company experienced lower levels of evaporation of its outbound cargoes with the more secure steel hatch.

The diesel message was getting through and Ross and Marshall's *Stormlight* of 1957 was planned as a motor vessel. However, the Iran oil crisis sent shivers of apprehension throughout the Western world, especially Greenock and Port Glasgow, and at the last moment management decided to revert to steam propulsion. She was converted later but that is another story.

The *Glenshira* experience was absorbed by Hamilton and McPhail and the operation of the *Pibroch* confirmed their own findings. They made ready for the next step – a ship that was not bound by the limits of any Scottish canal. The faster motor coasters, with a better hydrodynamic hull form, found the rounding of the Mull of Kintyre less of a hazard and no greater a problem than other exposed parts of the West Coast. The engineering inadequacies of the Crinan Canal had been apparent for many years. Frequent closures due to lack of water and hull damage suffered on the rocky sides and bottom at the narrow Crinan end were the main complaints. The question asked was whether the *Glenshira* prototype could be further improved to make the journey to the islands via the Mull and to ignore the doubtful virtues of the Crinan.

A hull longer than 88 feet could, if properly designed, mean greater speed (speed being proportional to the square root of the water-line length) and the operating range of the vessel could be extended. Greater cargo capacity, certainly above 200 tons deadweight, could be obtained. Also there could be better accommodation for a larger crew (up to six men) to discharge the larger cargoes in West Highland ports where there were no stevedoring facilities. The possibility of lower freight rates was even

Built in 1965, Hay-Hamilton's *Glenfyne* was the logical development of the diesel-engined ship which was not restricted by the need to use the Crinan Canal. She and her sister-ship, *Glencloy*, were, together with Ross and Marshall's *Dawnlight*, the last coasters of less than 200 g.r.t. specifically designed for the West Coast trade. They were also amongst the most aesthetically pleasing.

The launch of Ross & Marshall's MV *Dawnlight* in 1965. Clearly seen are the hatch board arrangement typical of the 1960s puffer and the 30 cwt capacity hydraulic crane. The split hatch caused some inconvenience and the 'Animal' as the crane was unaffectionately known to the crew, was found to be unreliable and was replaced. The hatch boards were numbered so that they could be placed in their correct positions to ensure, once covered with a tarpaulin, a watertight seal. It also saved time in placing the boards. Manhandling 180 hatch boards was a back breaking task for the crew, not just on this ship, but on all coasters of this era before the introduction of mechanically operated steel hatch covers.

mooted as a result of these efficiencies.

Freed from the restriction of the Crinan locks the coaster could easily have been developed into a ship of 100 to 120 feet

overall length and would still have fitted into most West Highland harbours. (By the 1960s beach cargoes had declined very significantly in number and were not taken into account in design considerations.) However there remained one important factor and that was the gross registered tonnage of the vessel. The Board of Trade in its various guises (Department of Transport, etc.) tended to think in paragraphs and owners often tended to build ships to fit these paragraphs. A paragraph in the regulations might well begin 'all vessels below 200 gross registered tons will be exempt from…'. Another might well deal with vessels between 200 and 499 g.r.t. (At one time the Chamber of Shipping, the British shipping industry's trade association, did not recognise as a ship any floating object below 500 g.r.t.) So the coaster owner came to regard 199.9 g.r.t. as the maximum size he would design. This meant that the vessel would be free of the administration of the then National Maritime Board manning scales, regulations about crews' hours and overtime and would be unlikely to attract the attention of trades unions.

There then emerged, during the period 1963 to 1966, a series of vessels which were to be the last to be designed specifically for the West Highlands. They were *Glensheil*, *Glenfyne*, *Dawnlight* and *Glencloy*. The last three were virtually clones, being 107ft overall, around 23ft in beam and with a loaded draft of 10ft. They carried 240 tons of cargo and had a service speed of 9.5 knots. Ross and Marshall's *Dawnlight* had a Crossley diesel while Hay-Hamilton favoured the Alpha engine of Burmeister and Wain. *Glensheil*, the first of the breed in 1963, was longer at 111ft and as narrow as *Dawnlight* at 22ft. Ross and Marshall had fitted a 2 ton Atlas hydraulic crane amidships, thereby splitting the 51ft long hatch. The others had hydraulic 3 ton capacity swinging derricks.

Above The hold of Ross and Marshall's *Dawnlight* in its pristine condition showing the frame spacing and the wooden ceiling. It looked very different after carrying a cargo of road salt.

Left The original crane having been found to be unreliable, *Dawnlight* is seen here having the newly fitted Speedcrane, supplied by the Hay-Hamilton subsidiary, put under load. Similar cranes which ran on gantry rails were installed on the two of the four 400 tonners that Glenlight bought in 1975. The other two were fitted with Jonserad cranes which specialised in log handling.

The Atlas was not a success and was replaced by a Speedcrane, purchased from Hay-Hamilton who had decided to diversify into cargo handling gear. *Glensheil*, was, due to an error on the part of the Registrar of Ships in Glasgow when transcribing the carving note, actually registered as two words as *Glen Sheil*, but this was fudged when the name was painted on the ship by using capitals throughout and

THE EVOLUTION OF THE PUFFER

The diagram opposite illustrates the evolution of the puffer over a period of approximately a century. It shows the relative proportions of the ship given over to propulsion, crew accommodation and cargo space. (They are also tabulated below as percentages.) Two trends emerge:

1) Crew accommodation progressively moves aft, first of all for the master only, from about 1900 onwards, until in the 1950s everybody is living at the stern and above the waterline.
2) The steering mechanism is moved on to the top of the engine room casing, first of all behind the lum, except in the case of the pre-World War 1 motor vessels (Because there is no lum.), and eventually to the fore in the 1950s versions. The steering was generally enclosed in a wheelhouse by the late 1930s.

Percentage Space

DATE		ENGINE	CREW	CARGO
1870	Steam	27	20	53
1900	Steam	30	15	55
1910	Motor	20	13	67
1950	Steam	37	10	53
1960	Motor	19	16	65

While the steam lighter of the 1950s had distinct improvements on its predecessors in terms of mechanical efficiency, sea-worthiness and crew comfort and while it had grown larger, within the limits imposed by the Crinan Canal, there has been little change in the relative proportions of space that were given over to the three main functional areas of engine, crew and cargo. If the individual areas are expressed as a percentage of their sum then the engine space is about 30% of the total, crew accommodation about 15% with the money earning cargo space unchanging over the years at 55%. On the other hand when the change is made to motor propulsion, whether in 1910 or in 1960, the cargo space rises to 65/67% of the total. This was the case for the 120 ton deadweight *Innisgara* class, built by McGregor at Kirkintilloch from 1912 onwards and for the 240 ton *Glenfyne* class of the 1960s. In this respect the comparison between the 1900/1910 steam and motor lighter is the most revealing about the advantages of the move from coal to diesel on the economics of the ships' operation. It is a great regret that nobody persevered with the 1912 experiment with motor propulsion.

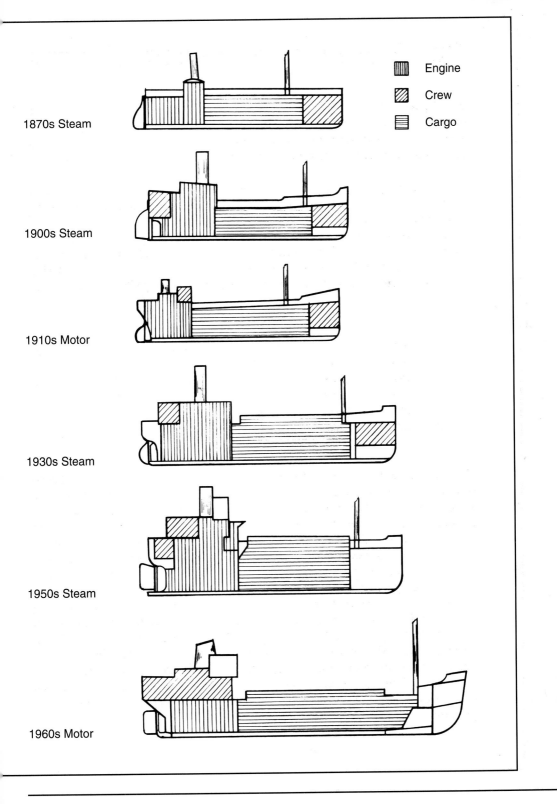

1870s Steam

1900s Steam

1910s Motor

1930s Steam

1950s Steam

1960s Motor

Engine

Crew

Cargo

placing the two words as close to each other as was possible. She was always referred to as *Glensheil*.

The curious tale of *Stormlight* remains to be told. Ross and Marshall soon regretted their panic decision to build her as a steamer and she became a bone of contention in the new company after the major interests amalgamated to form Glenlight in 1968. Under the influence of the ever adventurous Hamilton thinking, the decision was made to develop a hydraulic propulsion system. Hydraulics were necessary for the cargo gear and this was extended to include an auger in the hold for grain cargoes. Hay-Hamilton were knowledgeable in the field of hydraulic power packs (They had formed a subsidiary company to design and make hydraulic cargo gear.) and there was a superficial attractiveness in having an all hydraulic ship. Three inexpensive marinised Ford engines were installed to power hydraulic packs which then drove the propeller shaft. A speed of eight knots was achieved. But the system was in constant need of attention and was unreliable in inexperienced hands. As a result she was unpopular with crews. She stranded off Craighouse, Jura, in 1974 as a result of an engine failure, (the crew were saved), and became a total loss. The experiment was not repeated as there was little opportunity or indeed inclination.

Although, in the 1950/60s, neither Hay nor Hamilton had bought coastal vessels second-hand, Ross and Marshall had and the trend continued in the 1970s for Glenlight. As the pattern of operations changed and the VICs and smaller and older coasters aged or were lost, the search to find suitable replacement tonnage began. Upward spiralling ship-building costs, in that high inflation decade, precluded new purpose-built ships. The solution was found in the purchase of a fleet of five 400 ton deadweight vessels.

They offered economies of scale. It took the same five men and the same one ton of bunkers that drove *Glenfyne*'s 240 tons to move the larger tonnage. They could take 240 tons of ballast in their double-bottomed hulls and could therefore make better light-ship passages, an important feature in the West Highland trade where return cargoes were rare. Magically, they were under 200 g.r.t. However, they had no cargo gear and a single hold of a length that made the working of a single derrick impractical. Gantry cranes, which ran down the length of the ships on rails fitted on either side of the steel hatches, were installed. The ships had enough reserve of stability to take the extra top weight and the deadweight was reduced to about 340 tons as a consequence of fitting the cranes. Two were fitted with 3 ton Speedcranes and two with the more versatile 5 ton Jonserads which were well suited to the growing timber trade. Four entered the West Highland service as *Polarlight*, *Sealight*, *Glenrosa* and *Glenetive*. They were powered by 400 HP Rolls Royce marine diesel engines. The gantry crane concept was used on three further occasions when Glenlight, before its demise, acquired replacement tonnage and had to make it fit for the West Highlands.

The vessels lacked the aesthetic appeal of the *Glencloy* and *Dawnlight* class. They were Rolls Royces in only one sense. They had begun their lives as motorised Medway barges built for the cross Channel trades and with a low air draft for the Continental rivers and bridges. However they served their purpose well. Perhaps it was appropriate that a chain of technical change and development that began with the conversion of a barge ended in the same way, more than a century later.

The Hays and the Hamiltons

At some point in the 1830s William Hay, consciously or unconsciously, made the transition from being a farmer who owned canal scows to being a barge master who owned a farm. The Forth & Clyde Canal bordered his lands at Hillhead Farm, Kirkintilloch, and he kept a horse-drawn scow as part of his farm equipment for the movement of manure about his own and neighbours' holdings. No doubt he also met the transport needs of local quarries, collieries and sawmills as they grew up around the canal. Cleaning the hold between cargoes may not have been a requirement if the consumers of domestic coal had a high regard for the character of reek produced by William's cargoes.

Certainly he built barges in his own name from 1842 onwards and was registered as the owner of such until 1860. His eldest son, James, also became an owner of scows in 1851. Being experienced in the husbandry of horse power it was not necessarily difficult to make the transition to the canal if the scow was regarded as a water borne form of the familiar farm cart.

Judged by the revenues earned by the Forth & Clyde Canal Company for sea-to-sea carriage of goods, the 1830s were a period of growth for canal transport. This growth continued on through the 1850s and 1860s. The Hays had the good commercial sense to take advantage of these developments on their own doorstep. At this time Kirkintilloch was a busy 'port' serving the local coal, iron, timber and textile industries.

James saw his future outside farming because in 1857 (the year of the building of the *Glasgow* and a year after the successful *Thomas* experiment) he set up in business as a ships' agent, thus broadening the scope of what was presumably a prosperous concern. A younger brother, John, had gained marine engineering experience on Clydeside and would have

On the repair slip at Hays' yard, Kirkintilloch, in 1889, is *Delta*, one of their early 'outside' boats, built in 1881. The confidence in the steam engines of the day is demonstrated by the fact that she is rigged for sail, with both a gaff and a jib. (William Simpson Library, Kirkintilloch)

been sensible of the opportunities offered to the canal trade by the introduction of steam propulsion. It is possible, but not proven, that some of Hay's scows were converted to steam propulsion in the manner of the *Thomas* over the next ten years. They owned several steam lighters by 1867, the year in which a unique opportunity presented itself to the brothers.

They formed a partnership, known as J. and J. Hay, and took over the struggling co-operative shipbuilding venture, Crawford and Co. This company, based on the canal at Kirkintilloch, had built one composite, iron framed, wooden hulled lighter but had then run into financial difficulties. The Hays saw the opportunity to acquire a repair facility for their fleet and to build for their own account. The emphasis was always on repair work and they seldom built more than one barge or lighter a year. Nevertheless from 1869 to 1945 Hays built 64 vessels, 61 for themselves, and became a major force in the puffer trade.

The canal trade, served by the horse-drawn scows, remained a significant part of the Hay business for nearly a century and was the dominant feature in the early days. (At the end of the century they still owned forty barges and forty horses,) Gradually the steam lighter fleet grew, until the balance sheet for 1896, the year in which the partnership became incorporated as a limited liability company, shows fifteen of them. These were true canal boats of up to 66 ft in length, 18 ft beam and 8 ft draft with gross tonnages of between 35 and 85 tons.

The 1867 partnership agreement had ten year currency and by 1879, the year of his death, James Hay had gone off to develop a middle and deep sea trade with ships of up to 500 tons deadweight. It was known as the Strath Line and came under the management of James Hay and Sons.

J. & J. Hay was incorporated with a share capital of fifty thousand pounds, five thousand shares of ten pounds value being issued. John Hay had an eighteen percent holding and Sir William Beardmore was one of the directors, indicating that the company had a sound reputation in Scottish commercial circles. The accounts for the period make no distinction between the profits made from the steam lighters, barges and shipbuilding. Ships were incorporated in the balance sheet at their cost of building, however determined. It was blithely assumed, and it may even have been true, that it was cheaper to build than to buy from another builder. In 1902 they charged themselves £900 for ss *Greek* and two years later £1,200 each for the very similar *Roman* and *Saxon*. Profits for the period up to the Great War were around five thousand pounds annually. Most of this went on satisfying management commission (usually 2.5%), the requirements of preference shareholders and dividends of between ten and fifteen percent for holders of ordinary shares. There were the inevitable losses in the fleet through gales, strandings and founderings which were balanced by the director's 'one-new-lighter-a-year-from-the-yard' policy. Yet the 1914 balance sheet details the net assets of the company at £52,700, only some £2,700 more than the value at incorporation in 1896. Even in a period of no inflation a five percent growth in the value of the company is hardly spectacular in an eighteen year period. But of course the needs of capital had to be met by the payment of healthy dividends and in this respect the Hay shareholders were no different from their contemporaries.

A glimpse of the trading conditions at the turn of the century has come down to us through the survival of two scraps of paper (see p40). Mr. John Thom of Kirkintilloch, as owner of a quarter share in ss *Lyra* had her trading results for 1895

Hays' *Turk*, built 1900, a good example of a turn of the century lighter. (Scottish Maritime Museum)

reported to him in March 1896. She made £175 on a turnover of £1,153. No charge is made for depreciation and presumably Mr. Thom was expected to take the wear and tear on his asset into account when assessing the adequacy of the cheque for £44 as a return on his original investment. *Lyra* was an iron hulled steam lighter of 69 gross registered tons (say around 100 tons deadweight) built by Hay at Kirkintilloch in 1880. *Nelson* (built 1893 and slightly larger at 81 g.r.t) is known to have made £1,226 in the three years 1899 to 1901 on freight earnings of £4,479; a much better performance.

It was in the year of the launch of *Nelson* that Hay began what became their tradition of using tribal names for the ships that they built. *Briton* was the first, followed by *Celt*, *Saxon* and *Norman* in 1894 and 1895. *Chindit* was the last of the Kirkintilloch line in 1945.

Around this time another famous puffer name, *Glencloy*, was about to make its appearance out of Arran. Lying where it does in the mid Firth of Clyde this attractive island has bred sailors for hundreds of years. One family business, which had serviced the Arran islanders with many of the necessities of life for over thirty years, was that of Captain Adam Hamilton, whose father before him had been in the trade since 1828. Adam originally had a two masted topsail schooner, *Brodick*, but in 1895 he was about to make the logical transition from sail to steam.

He and his two sons, George and Gavin, who were eventually to become G. and G. Hamilton, worked away for three years, between trips to Ardrossan, building a wooden hull for a steam lighter. The chosen site for their 'yard' was at Brodick near the burns of Rosa and Cloy. The latter name prevailed and they called their ship *Glencloy*. She was at Arran and

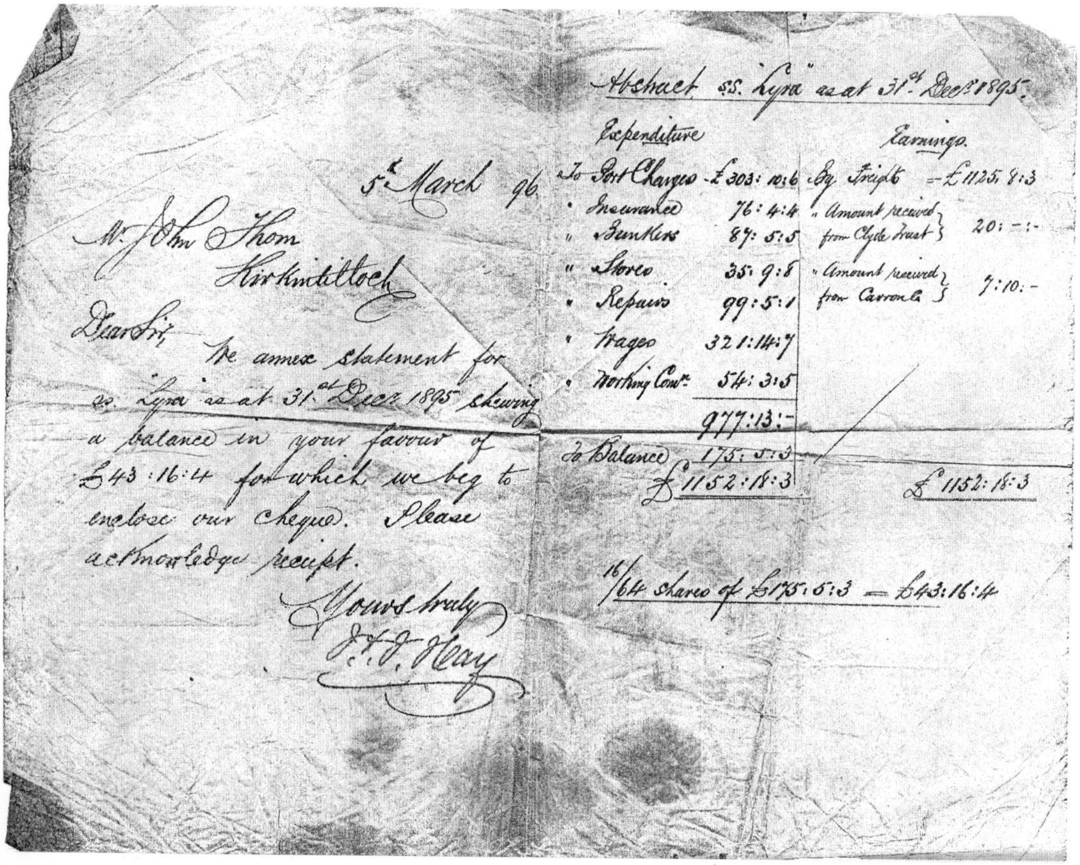

Abstract ss. "Lyra" as at 31st Decr 1895.

	Expenditure		Earnings	
To Port Charges	£303 : 10:6	By Freight	£1125 : 8 : 3
" Insurance	76 : 4:4	" Amount received from Clyde Trust	20 : - : -
" Bunkers	87 : 5:5	" Amount received from Carronla	7 : 10 : -
" Stores	35 : 9:8		
" Repairs	99 : 5 : 1		
" Wages	321 : 14:7		
" Working Contr	54 : 3:5		
	977:13:-		
To Balance	175 : 5:3		
	£1152 : 18:3		£1152 : 18:3

16/64 shares of £175 : 5:3 = £43:16:4

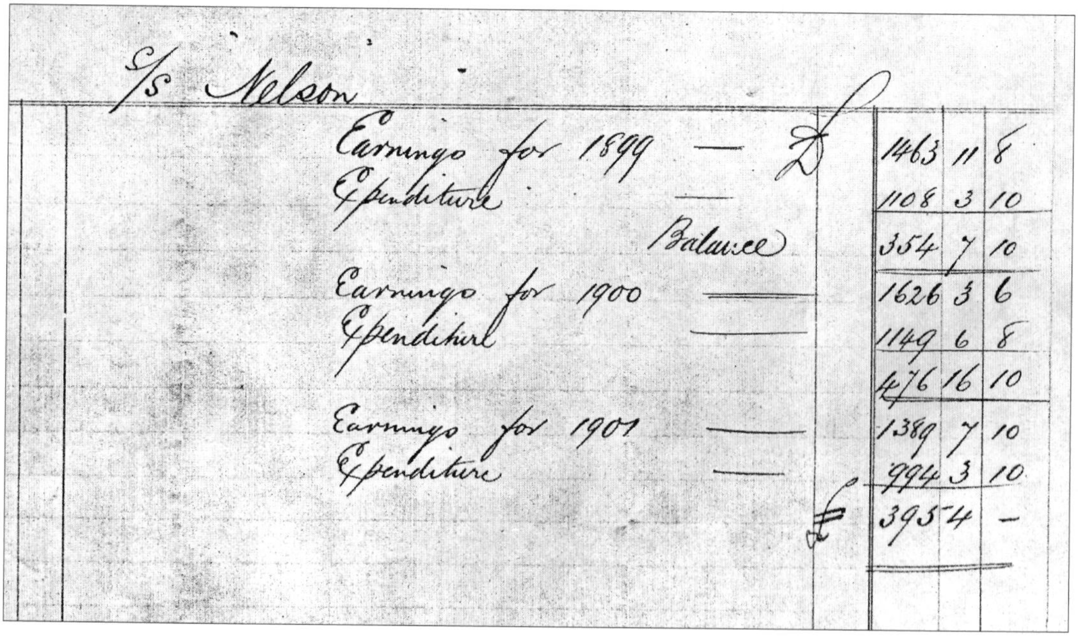

5 March 96

Mr John Thom
Kirkintilloch

Dear Sir
We annex statement for
ss. "Lyra" as at 31st Decr 1895 shewing
a balance in your favour of
£43 : 16 : 4 for which we beg to
enclose our cheque. Please
acknowledge receipt.

Yours truly
J & J Hay

P/s Nelson

	£	s	d
Earnings for 1899	1463	11	8
Expenditure	1108	3	10
Balance	354	7	10
Earnings for 1900	1626	3	6
Expenditure	1149	6	8
	476	16	10
Earnings for 1901	1389	7	10
Expenditure	994	3	10
£	3954	-	

her engine was in Glasgow. The tow to marry the two was paid for by a cargo of sand sold in Glasgow and they were in business. Had the Hamiltons been more experienced engineers and less experienced sailing masters they might have anticipated some of the problems their wooden hull would give them with the alignment of their tailshaft, which overheated badly from the first. They cured the problem by the simple expedient of removing the packing from the tailshaft gland and letting water leak in to cool down the shaft. They traded the *Glencloy* happily until 1911 and as far as we know

did not attempt to patent this revolutionary concept. Little is known of their commercial success or otherwise in those early days but clearly they did well enough to survive and develop. They built themselves up to a two ship operation when they ordered the *Invercloy*, with a steel hull this time, in 1904 from the Larne Shipbuilding Co. *Glencloy* was sold to Tralee interests in 1911 for £575 as the Hamiltons had taken delivery of *Rivercloy*, also from the Larne yard. She spent the first three years of her life taking materials and equipment to Kinlochleven for the bauxite smelter there. The refined aluminium often produced a southbound cargo to Glasgow.

The years of the First World War were some of the most profitable for J. & J. Hay, despite the closure of the Forth (and hence

The original *Glencloy* at her birthplace in the burn at Brodick, Arran. Her wooden hull was assembled here in 1895 and was then towed to Glasgow to have an engine fitted. She was the first of four of the name *Glencloy* owned by Glenlight Shipping and its antecedents.

Goatfell from Pier, Brodick.

RELIABLE SERIES

the canal to east coast traffic) because of the perceived threat from across the North Sea. However, lucrative contracts with the Admiralty, particularly for lighterage work for the ships of war at Rosyth, Invergordon and Scapa Flow, compensated for the loss of traditional work. (Indeed, the beginning of the decline of the Forth & Clyde may be traced to this period, as other considerations apart, it did not recapture its east coast traffic from the road and rail alternatives which developed during the War.) Hay's profits doubled between 1914 and 1918 and reached a remarkable £27,000 in 1920 (nearly five times those of 1913). The net worth of the company had increased by fifty per cent even though dividends as high as 22.5% were paid on the ordinary share capital!

Looking for economies of scale, the Hays decided to amalgamate the two branches of the family shipping interests under one management. What had originally been James Hay's Strath Line of large coasters, which had operated from 1890 as J. Hay and Son Ltd., bought out the shareholders of J. & J. Hay Ltd. The coasters and lighters then operated under the former name, a situation that was to pertain from 1921 until 1956.

Existing records do not make it easy to establish the profitability of the lighters, as distinct from the larger coasting fleet, during this period. It would seem to have been a period of little change, even of stagnation, as the freights earned annually by the lighters showed no pattern of sustained growth. (A turnover of £50,000 per annum would typify the 1920s and 1930s.) Approximately 60% of income was coming from the trading of the outside boats to the West coast and the islands, with the rest coming from the canal. As in the 1914–18 conflict, earnings rose significantly during the Second World War and even in the post-war period grew to a record £91,500 in 1957 before declining

to 1930s levels as the decade progressed. Appendix III provides a snapshot of the operating results of the outside boats for 1938 which are typical of the period.

Profits for the combined operation in the decade after World War II averaged around £50,000 per annum giving percentage returns on investment in the high teens. However the trend in profitability was downwards after 1951 and there is clear evidence that more investment was being made in the deep sea fleet in this period. This must have been a deliberate strategy as new-buildings could have been afforded from the healthy cash flow generated. A deal was struck in 1956 for the sale of these larger ships to the well established English shipping company F.T. Everard. The lighter business was retained. The Hays' judgement or instinct proved to be sound as for some years this section of the trade lost money under Everard's management and did not recover until well into the 1960s. Everard took the 'J. Hay and Sons Ltd' name with the ships and the 'J. and J. Hay Ltd' title was revived for Hays' continued interest in the West Highland trade.

Between the wars the Hamiltons had brought the second generation of *Glencloy* and *Invercloy* into the trade and in 1948 formalised their commercial relationship in Colin McPhail and Co. The McPhail company had built their first lighter *Gleannshira* at Scotts of Bowling, in 1903. (Note the full Gaelic spelling of the name. The River Shira runs into Loch Fyne at Inveraray and McPhail favoured Loch Fyne names for his ships.) The company survived as a one or two ship operation under the name, registered in 1932, of the Shira Steamship Co. Ltd. The Hamiltons were essentially skipper/owners and as such spent most of their time at sea and Colin McPhail became their designated ship manager. Cross shareholdings and directorships were set up between G. and

A Hay lighter at Scapa Flow in 1918. The deployment of part of Hays' fleet in Orkney in 1914–18 on service to the Admiralty did much to compensate for the loss of Forth & Clyde Canal traffic during the War. This picture is reproduced from a newspaper of the day and while the language of the report may seem extreme today it is difficult to remember at this remove what feeling the War stirred up.

PICKING UP THE RATS THAT LEFT THEIR SINKING SHIPS

Once more "violating all the decent laws and rules of the seas," Admiral von Reuter, in command of the German ships interned at Scappa Flow scuttled the German High Sea Fleet that had surrendered to the British Grand Fleet without striking a blow. Taking to the boats the German sailors waited, with hands uplifted and 'Kamerad!" on their lips, until British sailors came along and took them off to prison camps.

ss *Glencloy* (II) is seen here discharging into a lorry at Bunnahabain, Islay, with the cloud-shrouded Paps of Jura in the background. (D. MacDonald Collection)

G. Hamilton Ltd., the Shirra Steamship Co. Ltd. and Colin McPhail and Co. Ltd. They shared more than the prefix 'Glen' for naming their ships. With their practical seagoing background they proved to be the most forward thinking grouping, in technical terms, in the lighter business.

They, of course, produced the first diesel lighter, the *Glenshira* of 1953. Their first joint venture was the purchase in 1948 of VIC 89 which they upgraded and traded until 1964. They used another Loch Fyne name and called her *Glenaray*.

After the Hays had successfully extricated themselves from the middle sea trades they joined their lighter interest to an indifferently profitable coal merchanting operation in Dunoon. But as the 1950s drew to a close they faced other problems. They were doing little better than breaking even with their combined operation (in spite of positive contributions from the shipping) and they had a fleet of fifteen steam driven, and therefore obsolescent, coasters. There was considerable uncertainty over the future of the Forth & Clyde Canal and consequently of their Kirkintilloch yard. In 1959 they began a programme of converting their four newest ships (all 1938–47 vintage) to motor vessels. The loss of MV *Druid* in 1962, their last new building, and their first venture into the 200 ton class, was a serious set-back to their attempt to match their competitors' modern coasters. (She capsized, with the loss of her crew, in circumstances that were never explained satisfactorily.) Trade on the Forth & Clyde Canal had withered after 1946 and its owners scheduled it for closure on 1st January 1963. In anticipation of this the Kirkintilloch yard was closed in December 1962. The Hays had of course built outside the Canal, specifically at Scotts, but they had stuck to the Forth & Clyde design with its limit of 130 tons deadweight. Ross and Marshall and Hamilton-McPhail were building to at least Crinan limits and achieving cargo capacities of 180 to 200 tons deadweight. Even with diesel engines Hays' ships were going to be just too small to compete economically. As a result they sought a partnership with Hamilton-McPhail and were not rebuffed.

The 1964 deal absorbed the Hamilton-McPhail companies into J. & J. Hay and the name of Hay-Hamilton was adopted. The Hays had the stronger balance sheet but the less valuable fleet in terms of age and technology. Hamilton-McPhail were able to cash in some of their capital and Hamilton retained 21.5% of the new company. (McPhail retired at the end of 1965.)

The five Hamilton-McPhail ships were the heart of the new balance sheet value of £164,000. The trading strength was also in the five Hamilton ships, two of which were diesels, and they had a new building on order, the 1965 *Glenfyne* of 240 tons deadweight. All of Hay's 130 ton deadweight steamers were broken up and their contribution to the amalgamation was four diesel conversions each of 130 tons deadweight.

Hay-Hamilton became attractively

In both World Wars the lighters performed many unrecorded duties in great ports around the world trans-shipping the materials of war. Here ss *Perfection*, built at McGregor's yard at Kirkintilloch in 1916, and therefore a veteran of both Wars, is seen alongside HMS *Hecla* in 1942.

Hays' last new-building on their own account, the 240 ton deadweight MV *Druid*. She was the last to bear one of the famous tribal names and was unusual even for a modern puffer in having a twin derrick system. She was tragically lost with her crew in 1962 and thereafter Hay built under the Hay-Hamilton names using the 'Glen' prefix.

profitable in the 1964–67 period with an average return of 9.5% on their assets even after the impact of the investment in 1965/6 of £124,000 in the new ships *Glenfyne* and *Glencloy*. The new company presented a formidable face to its opposition by the end of 1966 with its all diesel fleet of eight coasters. Nevertheless they were keeping a wary eye open for developments at their main opposition, Ross and Marshall, which had been acquired in 1963 by Clyde Shipping Co. Ltd. Indeed the fact that their rival was owned by a company of the perceived strength of Clyde Shipping had influenced Hamilton's and Hays' decision to amalgamate. They considered that they needed financial stability and their combined size to compete.

Feelers were put out from time to time to ascertain Clyde's intentions for its new lighter business but Clyde was too preoccupied getting to grips with the ramifications of Ross and Marshall's widespread interests to respond adequately. The lines of communications were well established as the various lighter companies frequently chartered each other's tonnage to meet the peaks of demand for cargoes and both companies had knowledge of the freight rates charged by each other. Hay-Hamilton were reaping the benefit of their investment in newer ships and their policy of not increasing freights was construed by Ross and Marshall as akin to rate-cutting.

Hay-Hamilton were not aware of the pressures that Clyde was coming under through their own efforts and extraneous factors. So that when Ross and Marshall made an informal approach in late 1966 seeking a form of 'co-operation' between the trade's two largest companies Hay-Hamilton responded positively but very cautiously.

A scene from the 1953 film 'The Maggie', the story of the tribulations of a puffer skipper/owner. The incident was based on an actual accident in which Warnock's *Faithful* grounded at low water on the tunnel of Glasgow's Underground.

Hays' two lighters, *Boer* and *Inca*, were used for much of the filming although a mock-up was employed for this scene. The attention to detail is commendable; in real life the ship's mast would have been lowered to allow her to pass the bridges on the upper river. The part of the skipper of the 'Maggie' was played by Alexander Mackenzie, who was born in Kirkintilloch, like *Boer* and *Inca*.

Warnock's ships had another tenuous claim to cinematic fame. They were employed on the salvage of the *Politician*, on the stranding of which Compton Mackenzie based his novel 'Whisky Galore'. This was subsequently filmed, directed by Alexander Mackendrick, as was 'The Maggie'. (National Film Archive)

Ross and Marshall

Before the days of the dredging of the Clyde and the development of the railways, Greenock and Port Glasgow were the lighterage harbours for Glasgow. Deep sea vessels could not venture up the shallow muddy Clyde and Port Glasgow was literally the port of the city of Glasgow. In the 1850s two of the many thriving lighterage businesses in the area were that of Alexander Ross, who was also a coal merchant, and James Marshall, who in addition was a haulage contractor and a stevedore. They had both used steam for the winches on their dumb barges, particularly for the transhipment of timber, and quickly saw the logic of the use of steam for propulsion that was being developed for the barges on the Forth & Clyde Canal. Both had moved in that direction before 1872, the year in which they decided to amalgamate their interests and set up the partnership of Ross and Marshall with offices in Greenock.

Some records have survived from 1879 and they show the company involved in lighterage (with steam and sail powered vessels), stevedoring (of sugar and timber), cartage, coal merchanting (Welsh coal for the Royal Navy at Greenock and Lamlash), engineering, shipbuilding and salvage. In such a diverse business, with a singular approach to accounting, few conclusions can be drawn about the prosperity of the lighterage. That it was the core of the business there is little doubt and it survived down the years after other aspects of the original business died off. Given the lack of sentimentality of the Victorians in money matters and the fact that they invested in and developed this aspect of the company it can be assumed safely that the lighters created added value. (Appendix IV gives details of the 1882 profits.)

The Ross and Marshall shipbuilding enterprise did not mirror that of the Hays on the Forth & Clyde. For much the same reasons as those of the Hays – the repair and maintenance of their own fleet, R&M developed a slipway and engineering facility at Main Street, Greenock. They are credited with building fourteen ships and steam yachts between 1899 and 1925 when the yard was sold to Scotts' of Greenock. For R&M, unlike the Hays, there was no shortage of alternative shipbuilding and repair companies in their immediate geographic area. They had ships constructed, for example at Ferguson Bros. (Port Glasgow) Ltd. and at 'Siberia', as the yard of G. Brown & Co. (Marine) Ltd. was known because of its exposure to cold northerly winds. Their own yard continued the tradition of producing 'light' names such as *Moonlight*, *Starlight* and *Warlight* which were the hallmark of R&M down through the years. Occasionally when inspiration ran out the company did resort to 'ite' as in Chrysolite (magnesium-iron silicate) and even to 'yte' as in *Acolyte*, having exhausted the possibilities of *Electriclight*, *Searchlight* etc. (Incidentally, *Acolyte* was in service for fifty-one years, going to the breaker's yard in 1936.)

The annual accounts for 1879 put a value of £12,000 on the concern but, coyly, do not report the profit for the year. Profits were recorded from 1882 onwards and reached a high of £8,674 in 1898 before the company plunged into the red between 1900 and 1902. The cause was not any worsening of trading conditions

Ross and Marshall's yard and slip at Main Street, Greenock, in the 1890s. The company occupied this site, which lay roughly half way between the Victoria Harbour and the James Watt Dock, until 1925 when it was sold to Scotts' of Greenock and incorporated in their Cartsdyke complex. Various lighters of different vintages are to be seen with the vessel on the slip having a steering wheel and that at the jetty having a tiller. We may conclude from this evidence that the former was one of the larger 'outside' boats.

but the recognition that perhaps they ought to be charging depreciation before declaring a profit. Five percent of the value of the ships was debited from the profit and loss statement from 1900 onwards. Whatever adjustments were made by way of price increases or internal economies, they returned to the black in 1903 with a profit of £2,971.

Dividends of about 5% per annum were normally paid on what the accounts described as 'the capital account' of each partner (See Appendix IV). This capital account had been their original investment in the partnership and had grown to the extent that profit was not wholly distributed. That they did retain cash in the business for its development is evidenced by the growth of the net assets to around £53,500 by the end of 1906.

The decades on either side of 1900

Two lighters have been lashed together to carry four tramcars. An early example of Ross and Marshall's 'Go anywhere carry anything' policy. The lighter on the left could be the *Arclight*. Two sail-rigged R and M vessels can be seen in the background. Rothesay, on the Isle of Bute once had a tramway system and the cars may have been bound there. Presumably this lash-up was towed to its destination.

were a period of rapid growth in the number of limited liability companies in Scotland. The crash of the Bank of Glasgow gave a terrifying example of what could happen to shareholders in an association of unlimited liability, and many successful businessmen saw the sense of establishing a legal separation of personal and corporate wealth. In March 1907 the partnership became Ross and Marshall Ltd. with its registered office at 28 Main Street, Greenock. The company paid the partners £53,500 for the property at Main Street, plant, goodwill and a fleet of thirty-three vessels. Of these there were '...five steamships, seventeen steam lighters and eleven miscellaneous craft' which were valued at £36,300. At this time the Ross family became the major shareholder subscribing £26,970 towards the new share issue to Marshall's £7,750.

The company continued on its profitable way up to and beyond the First World War, making significantly higher profits during the war as the demand for lighterage services, to the Royal Navy for example, increased. But there had been a significant change prior to the outbreak of hostilities. James Marshall, who had suffered poor health for some time, died in May 1913. Alexander Ross, who had been in business with Marshall for forty years and who was then over seventy, decided, at this point, that he wished to retire and looked around for a buyer. He found one in William Campbell, who was a successful Port Glasgow coal merchant and Chairman of Wm Campbell Ltd. He and his son Hugh became the principal shareholders and directors of the company.

By 1920 the company was concentrating its energies on coal sales, stevedoring and of course shipping and decided to venture outside the lighter trade. Two 800 ton deadweight ships were built for a total £102,000 to trade within what became familiar as the Elbe-Brest limits. In preparation for this, nearly £10,000 was raised from the sale of smaller older ships and the new ships *Raylight* and *Arclight* began trading in 1921. A new company was formed, the Light Shipping Co. Ltd. as a subsidiary of Ross and Marshall to trade these two new vessels and the residual twelve ships. Half of the share capital of £65,000 was owned by R&M and the Campbell family held thirty five per cent of the equity. The timing of this venture could not have been worse. Not for nothing is this 1920s period

known as the Depression. Trading conditions got very bad very quickly and losses were made. Perhaps because of their military background, William and Hugh Campbell decided to lead from the front and reduced the salaries of the directors in 1922. (William declined, as Managing Director, to be paid anything at all.)

It was not until 1923 that salaries and wages to staff were frozen. This situation was to last until 1927 when trade had sufficiently improved to allow modest increases to be paid. The 800 tonners were sold in 1933, not exactly having been a resounding success, and R&M did not again venture into the middle sea trades but stuck firmly to the lighter business.

Confidence had improved enough by 1933 to order a new vessel from Ferguson Brothers of Port Glasgow at a cost of £4,200 and a sister ship in 1935 for £3,800. These were typical canal boats of 66 feet overall length and a deadweight capacity of 110 tons. Similar fleet replacements followed in 1936 for £4,600 and in 1938 when an 88 ft Crinan type cost £6,300. These orders suggest that trading conditions had improved enough for the owner to judge that he could get an adequate return on an investment programme of nearly £15,000 in three years. The prices also go some way to explaining why R&M, and others in the trade, jumped at the chance of buying VICs for around £4,500 each when the Admiralty was selling them off in the immediate post-war period.

It is a curiosity of this period that none of the R&M vessels was insured prior to 1937. Strictly speaking they were self-insured as the company had built up an Insurance Reserve into which it dipped to pay for accidents and casualties. Luckily there were no major losses that might have wiped out the fund and presented the company with a serious financial problem. The puffer owner's attitude was that insur-

The *Sealight* of 1907 was a typical example of Ross and Marshall's Crinan size coaster which was intended for West Highland rather than Forth & Clyde traffic.

ance premiums were too high and an unwarranted expense. Such attitudes also prevailed at Hays in the early days, but they had reached the conclusion much earlier, certainly by the time of their reconstruction in 1921, that insurance made good sense. The modern ship manager would not contemplate going to sea without adequate insurance cover for his hull, machinery and a myriad of third party risks. At any rate the reserve was cancelled in 1937 and marine underwriters took on the risk at an appropriate price. Like many converts Hugh Campbell became an enthusiast and the company advanced him a loan so that he could become a member of a Lloyd's syndicate.

In World War II the Ross and Marshall business expanded beyond all recognition. Behind the anti-submarine boom at the Tail-of-the-Bank in the Clyde, a huge number of cargo, troop and warships assembled for convoy and other duties. There was insufficient quay space for them and they had to be serviced afloat. Under the direction of the Ministry of Transport the company controlled a truly complex fleet of over two hundred barges and eleven associated tugs, thirty eight steam lighters and twenty two specialised water carriers to cater for the needs of these ships. It is reputed that the company carried over two hundred million gallons of water, a commodity of which Greenock has never been short, between 1939 and 1946. In this period of hyper-activity the company was able to pay dividends averaging 7.5% to its shareholders.

The decade after the war was one of Ross and Marshall's most prosperous peace-time periods. The fleet was renewed by the purchase of two VICs and by ordering three new-buildings, the third of these, the ss *Moonlight,* of 180 ton deadweight, built at Northwich to Crinan limits. In addition the Campbell family's coal merchant company was taken over in its totality. Their equity holders were undoubtedly happy with their 20% dividend in 1956. At this time the company had two main activities apart from the ships. It was by now the only stevedoring company left in Greenock with British Oil and Cake Mills and Elders and Fyffes as its main customers. The great days of coal merchanting to the Royal Navy had declined with the decline of the use of steam for marine propulsion. However Wm Campbell Ltd. still enjoyed a substantial trade in domestic coal especially to the West Highlands. And of course owning a coal merchant secured the cargoes for the coasters. This simple view of what today is called vertical integration led R&M to 'support' and eventually acquire as subsidiaries Neil Beaton Ltd. of Portree, a large coal merchant on Skye, and the Eglinton Limestone quarries at Glenarm and Carnlough on the Antrim coast. This latter company supplied large quantities of limestone for the basic steel-making process in Lanarkshire and R&M gave its support on the condition that R&M had the exclusive right to carry the limestone cargoes. This process of creeping acquisition began in 1955 when

To get to Customs House Quay in the heart of Glasgow the lighters had to lower their derricks, and sometimes their lums, to pass the city bridges. Here R. & M.'s *Stormlight* (built 1933) is seen proceeding down river opposite the cupola of the Clyde Port Authority offices, at Robertson St., Glasgow. (D. MacDonald Collection)

Seen here on her trials on the Mersey in 1952, the *Moonlight* was Ross and Marshall's third post-War newbuilding and a traditional West Coast steamer. Yarwood's yard at Northwich, Cheshire, was chosen as the builder for this ship and the 1957 *Stormlight. Moonlight* had a deadweight of 170 tons and was designed with the Crinan Canal in mind. Within a year Hamilton and McPhail were to revolutionise the puffer world with their diesel engined *Glenshira.*

the shipping operation was performing well, but Eglinton put the whole company under strain. When Eglinton made substantial losses in the 1960-62 period the Light Shipping Company itself was taken into the red even though the vessels traded profitably, though not spectacularly so.

By 1962 Hugh Campbell had been a Director of R&M for forty eight years and its Chairman since 1926, the year of his father's death. He decided he wished to retire and sought a buyer for the whole company. He found one in Clyde Shipping Company, long established as tug-owners on the Clyde (since 1815 under various ownerships), and a company seeking to diversify after the dramatic decline of its main business, a century old coastal liner service. The sale of R&M was concluded in May 1963 and the company became a subsidiary of Clyde Shipping and J & J Denholm, who were primarily interested in the stevedoring business. (Clyde initially owned 74% of R&M and subsequently bought Denholm out in 1972.) Under Clyde's ownership the constituent parts of R&M were to have varied fortunes (after a difficult period in the 1960s Eglinton's development played a large and profitable role in Clyde) but we must concentrate on the Light Shipping Company.

Trading conditions were difficult in the early 1960s with low profits being made on the ships. Competition was fierce. The new owners decided not to pay a dividend and at one of their early board meetings decided that they had to make an approach to Hay-Hamilton about 'the current freight war'. The first steps were about to be taken that would lead to the formation of Glenlight Shipping; the 'lights' and the 'glens' were soon to come together.

In the 1960/70s Ross and Marshall kept their fleet capacity up with second hand purchases to complement their new ships MV *Raylight* (1962, 180 dwt.) and MV *Dawnlight* (1965, 240 dwt.). MV *Polarlight* was one such. She was built in 1959 as the MV *Queensgate*, and her 350 dwt. proved very useful on the West Coast. (D. MacDonald Collection)

Glenshiel is here loading limestone at Ross and Marshall's quarry at Glenarm, N. Ireland. Among its many uses, limestone (calcium carbonate) was frequently spread on fields to correct the acidity of the soil. An interest in the quarry was first acquired by Ross and Marshall in 1955 as a means of securing the rights to its cargoes.

Ross and Marshall's *Raylight* was built in 1962 at Scotts' of Greenock and was that company's answer to the move towards diesel propulsion in the West Highland trade. (The opportunity to 'go diesel' had been there when they build *Stormlight* in 1957 but a last minute decision to use steam was made.) At 96 feet overall and 170 dwt she was not a 'canal boat' and in a sense was the prototype for her larger 240 dwt sister, the *Dawnlight* of 1965, to which she bore a considerable resemblance.

3

THE TRADE

Beaches and Ports

The classic image of the puffer in the public mind is that of, say, the *Roman* high and dry on the Kilchattan Bay beach with cargo being handled overside (below). As

can be seen from this photograph, with the large rocks in the foreground, taking the ground was not without its dangers. It certainly was not a practice that was undertaken lightly.

A wealth of experience, trial and tribulation built up over many years went into the gentle art of beaching. Piers, of course, were preferred for the discharge of cargo, but in the service of many small Western communities it was essential to take ship and cargo as close to the user as possible. In many such places harbours were non-existent and roads were poor. The flexibility of being able to sail the ship into the heart of the village was its greatest advantage over other forms of transport. In this the lighter followed where the gabbert had led.

In all of this the lighter manager's bible was the Beach Book. Kept and updated over many years it was a veritable encyclopedia of the trade. It contained an alphabetical listing of obscure (to the landsman) points on the coasts of Scotland and Ireland, how to approach them and at what state of the tide, whether the ship could lie safely afloat or aground, who the local pilot was (if he existed) and what the harbour dues and cargo discharging rates were. Characteristically it was enlivened by comments such as

J. & J. Hay's *Roman* (built at Kirkintilloch in 1902) on the beach at Kilchattan Bay, Bute loading barrels of potatoes.

ss *Glencloy* is here seen in a remote Highland 'harbour' and this illustrates what tight corners the ships traded to. The nearest road is up by the tree line. The simple concrete wall obviously dries out at low water and there is a complete lack of navigational aids. In situations like this the skill and experience of the master was all important. (D. MacDonald Collection)

Below G. & G. Hamilton's *Rivercloy* of 1910. Note the open wheelhouse with provision for a canvas dodger. A cargo of bricks is being unloaded at a Highland pier, which unusually for that part of the world, has a small hand operated cargo winch.

X marks the Spot. This postcard was sent to the Ross and Marshall office by a skipper to report his location and progress in July 1937 and was placed in the Beach Book for future reference for Loch Broom. His report is reproduced below.

'This is not a safe place. Great difficulty in getting clear after getting afloat'. Thus spake one master in 1934 of Sanna on the Ardnamurchan peninsula. From Drummore (Mull of Galloway) to Miavaig (Harris) and Scourie (Sutherland, early closing Wednesday) to Killyleagh (Strangford Lough) the details were recorded for the safe and economic operation of the ships.

The principal and practical decoration of the Beach Book was postcards of the locations. The picture of Loch Broom (opposite) posted 8th July, 1937 has, on the other side, the message: 'The x is about the mark where we are beached. It is a fine beach and cargo can be worked for 6 hours. They were late in coming to us this morning and we are just finished now, 4 p.m. Willie'.

This postcard, to the Ross & Marshall office, was the most practical method of reporting for the master, either because there was no convenient phone or because

he was reluctant to use it. Before the days of the distinction between first and second class mail, a postcard could be in Glasgow the next day. How much more quickly did the office need to know anyway? Post Offices always had phones and their masters or mistresses could always be relied upon to look out the window, when requested by the worried ship manager, to see if the 'such-and-such' was lying at the pier. Crews could be persuaded to use Post Offices on those Fridays when the Glasgow office had arranged to have them pay out the wages. The view of Scarinish, on Tiree, (below), shows what, in the form of a simple stone jetty, passed for a West Highland harbour. The card records that

Scarinish, Tiree. The lighters had to negotiate the narrow entrance, which is exposed to the East and South, and swing sharply to starboard to lie inside the simple stone pier. The tide is out in the picture and it can be judged just how little water the master had in which to manoeuvre. The lack of any harbour facilities demonstrates why the true puffer had to be self-discharging.

SCARINISH HARBOUR, TIREE.

'*Moor* discharged there on Monday' The Beach Book comments of Scarinish: 'Spring tides needed. Bad with Southerly gale only.'

If at the stone slip at Ardlussa (Jura), 'a 120 ton boat should be able to berth with 50 tons of cargo (drawing 8' aft and 4½' ford) at the top of springs', the master was then aware of the difficulties of the place and of course the freight rate had to recover all the operating costs on only 50 tons of cargo. But sixty years ago the fifteen miles from Craighhouse to Ardlussa was along a single track road, as it is today, but then there was little motorised transport. It was just as well to sail another two hours up the coast and put the cargo exactly where it was wanted, with less fuss and expense.

The entry for Glengorm (Mull) gives a hint of that rare opportunity in the West Highland trade, the return cargo. 'Coal for the castle is discharged at the jetty at Loch na Ladnair. Timber is loaded on the beach (Good). Safe any winds'. Not to have to come South lightship for the next cargo was the shipowner's dream. If the castle and nearby forests were under one owner-ship no doubt there were deals to be done for the round trip.

There was more to the trade than romantic, Hebridean silver strands. There were 'proper' harbours that were frequently used by the coasters. They were on both the East and the West coast of Scotland as well as Northern Ireland. There are entries for Aberdeen, Montrose and Kirkcaldy to remind us that the puffers were not just West Coast traders. To approach Newry (Carlingford Lough, N. Ireland) in 1934, it was recorded by the master of the *Cretan* 'It is not necessary to lower funnel or mast to get to Buttercrane Quay.' It cost ten shillings each way for 'hobbling' (having the bridges opened) and in addition to the canal dues, one shilling had to be paid to the Hospital Fund. This was in the days before the National Health Service.

It is incredible today to consider that between Glasgow city and Campbeltown there were approximately 80 piers and jetties for passengers and cargo, if all the sea lochs in the Clyde river and estuary are included in the count. This was the case just prior to World War I when country roads were poor and the internal combustion engine had made little impact. MacBrayne introduced their first bus service in 1907, but it was not until after World War II that road transport seriously threatened the steam lighter's usefulness to the West's isolated communities.

Entries for 1933 in one Beach Book, show the discharging costs for ten different cargoes, for places like Campbeltown and Dunoon. They range from the inevitable coal to bricks and petrol. Harbour dues at Campbeltown were five old pence (the same as at Larne). These were paid according to the gross registered tonnage of the vessel. A typical 66ft boat would have a g.r.t of 95 and would therefore pay the harbour authority just under two pounds per visit. Since it cost a shilling or 5p per ton to discharge cement at Brodick pier and only half that amount if the ship berthed in the burn, we can now understand why all the photographs of the period show coasters at the burn (see p41 or colour p2).

The use made of the then still open Forth & Clyde Canal, by the lighters is to be seen in references to Grangemouth, Methil and Bo'ness. Maryhill rates are detailed, presumably for canal trade from the east, bound for Glasgow. Rates for even shorter voyages within the boundaries of Glasgow, from St. Rollox to Firhill for example, are quoted. Two shillings and four pence (say 11p) was the price per ton for keeping the movement of coal off the city streets.

Strangely there is only one entry for

Tarbert. Glued to the facing page is a postcard of Harris but considering the opportunity for confusion with the Tarberts of Loch Fyne, Jura and even of Loch Nevis and the tendency for skippers to get just a little absent-minded sometimes, this reader expected to see several destinations detailed. Certainly one master who docked at Port Ellen rather than, as instructed, at Port Askaig, forcibly pointed out, when taken to task for his error, that they were at least on the same island, 'No like Port Said.'

Just occasionally there was neither a pier nor a suitable beach for cargo discharge. In these cases cargo was transferred to shore by means of intermediary 'flit' boats. The coaster anchored as near to shore as was safe and small boats served as lighters to the lighter taking the goods to waiting shore transport. The illustration on page 64 shows such an operation using what looks like a dumb barge controlled by hand lines as the go-between. Unfortunately neither ship, (possibly Hamilton's *Rivercloy*?), nor location can be clearly identified.

Beaching continued almost up to the last days of the coasters. As roads improved and road transport extended its area of operation and as the ships became larger, the frequency of beach discharging declined. However the smaller islands clung to the tradition and the annual mixed cargo (everything including the kitchen sink) to Iona was the highlight of the summer trade well into the 1980s.

Those who 'know' Scotland's West Coast will have no difficulty in locating the places on the following list without resorting to a gazetteer:

Eoligarry	Kerrycroy
Port-na-long	Drimin
Aros	Kentallen
Petersport	Rhunahaorine

Hays' *Zephon*, built 1901 at Scott's of Bowling, beached for discharge. The photograph is taken from a postcard, with the company's stamp in the top left corner, a frequently used form of communication. Shipping companies often had postcards made up from pictures of their vessels as a form of publicity.

Above: Where no jetty existed it was not always possible to beach the lighter to discharge. Here we see what is obviously a well established local practice of rafting the cargo from the ship to the waiting land transport. In other places it was done in small boats known as 'flit boats'. The ship in question is probably G. & G. Hamilton's the *Rivercloy.*

Coming or Going? *Spartan* is beached in Loch Sunart. Has the Land Rover driver arrived early to take full advantage of the receding tide to remove his cargo? Is he taking a chance of being submerged by the incoming flood in an effort to wring the last drop of working time from the day?

Those who have to look them up will learn something of just how far the coaster ranged to serve Highland and Island communities. All these places had published freight rates into the late 1950s and certainly coal was being delivered to them up until then. Where are they? In the Beach Book, of course!

1

Above The 19th-century financial reports of Ross and Marshall always had an entry for salvage income but in this case we see two of Hays' ships, *Serb* and *Cretan*, engaged in the raising of one of Clyde Shipping Co. Ltd.'s tugs. In 1938 *Flying Spray* was holed by the propeller of the ship she was towing and sank in the Clyde. Beams connect *Serb* and *Cretan* and they are positioned over the wreck, the black funnel of which is partly obscured by the mast and derrick of *Serb*. The tug was raised progressively on each high tide by the buoyancy of these lighters and two others not pictured here. As they rose, tackle passed under the tug lifted her. (D. MacDonald Collection)

Below Hays commissioned Francis R. Flint (1915–1976), son of the famous watercolourist Sir William Russel Flint, to produce studies of the lighters at work, and he sailed on the ships to absorb their unique atmosphere.

2

3

Above On a glorious summer day in 1976 the 1965 *Glenfyne* is seen here discharging at Broadford, Skye.

Below The *Invercloy* of 1935 at the burn at Brodick. This was a safe and recognised berth and one used constantly by the lighters as the harbour dues were only half those charged for berthing at the pier.

4

5

Above *Glenfyne* at at Ramsey, Isle of Man. The second and last vessel to bear this name, she was originally *Lille Birgit*, built in 1989 in Denmark; after having a crane fitted she could carry 400 tons of cargo.

Below *Dawnlight* (built in 1965, 240 dwt), the last coaster specifically designed for the West Highlands by Ross and Marshall.

6

7 8

9

10

Top left Here we see logs being discharged from timber lorries directly on to the barge without the double handling inherent in transport by traditional coaster.

Top right *Sprucelight*, with a deadweight capacity of 600 tons, was the first barge designed by Glenlight for the transport of timber from remote Highland forests. The articulated ramp for vehicle access on beaches was a prominent feature in the success of the design.

Above Timber cargoes, before the advent of the tug and barge configuration, were double handled because of the need to store enough logs on a quay to justify a ship coming in to pick up an economic load.

Left An hydraulic crane and log grab in action loading a coaster with timber stacked on the quayside.

Real 'Para Handy' Tales

To paraphrase a much used quotation, 'The puffers made Para Handy and Para Handy made the puffers.' It is said that the Scots' affection for these small ships is due to the long lasting popularity of Neil Munro's tales. That has to be a Lowland view. For the Highlander and Islander, whatever sentiment they held for these coasters, they knew that they were a vital link with external markets.

Under the name of 'Hugh Foulis', Neil Munro wrote the Para Handy tales as occasional pieces in the *Glasgow Evening News*. Most were written between 1905 and 1923, although he composed only a handful after World War I. Anthologies were published in 1906, 1911 and 1923 and they have not been out of print since. They inspired television plays and at least one film, 'The Maggie'. They are the source of the general public's view of the puffer trade being a type of cruising holiday in some of the world's most spectacular scenery, and the pufferman being a genial imbibing care-free individual, not overly concerned about commercial matters. This is a picture that owes more to the imagination than to reality. What were Neil Munro's sources for these tales and characters? As a boy on Loch Fyneside, born in 1863, he would have seen the emergence of the steam lighter. As a journalist in Greenock and Glasgow up to 1902, when he began to devote himself to writing novels, he would have seen puffers almost daily. The greater number of the Para Handy tales belong to this period of his semi-retirement from newspaper work before he returned to a full time position on the *Glasgow Evening News* during the Great War. However something more than a general awareness of the ships and their crews was needed to compose the tales.

The oral tradition in Hays was that Munro used to frequent certain Glasgow riverside hostelries known to be favoured by the puffer crews. No aspersions are cast on the journalistic profession as a body, but they have had the reputation of needing to refresh themselves after the stress of meeting a deadline. So it is at least possible that Munro was not a Rechabite. Probably, in an atmosphere of good fellowship, conversations were struck up and turned to life at sea. No doubt tales were told which lost nothing in the telling in the conviviality of the occasion. Just possibly, Mr. Munro would be sought out by the more imaginative and thirsty argonauts knowing that he was an attentive and generous listener. Equally possibly quite ordinary people and occurrences were taken up by the talented and creative writer who transmuted them into printed gold. More than likely Para Handy and his crew actually existed as composites of several personalities. And of course all the stories were the plain unvarnished truth. As a dedicated newspaper reporter Mr. Munro would not have dreamt of gilding the lily.

There was a deep well of stories in Glenlight which it would be unwise to relate here. Not all of them, even the funniest, would have shown those ashore and afloat in the best light of the romantic '*Vital Spark*' tradition. And of course there are the laws of libel to consider for many of the *dramatis personae* still survive to this day. While there was an essential truth to many, but not necessarily all of these tales, each raconteur had his own variation and it often became difficult to decide at what point a story became apocryphal. Human nature being what it is, seldom were the sad and tragic tales, of which there were more than a few, told. While imitation is the sincerest form of flattery, the author of Para Handy needs no praise from us. The skills required to tell such tales must be regarded as uniquely Neil Munro's.

'During a storm at the end of last week the *Tiree* ran on the rocks in the south channel of the narrows in the Kyles. She was running light from Tiree at the time.'

The date and source of this newspaper clipping are not known. However *Tiree* was built in 1907 by Scotts at Bowling for C. & J. Lamont of Tiree. The Kyles referred to are presumably the Kyles of Bute, the narrow scenic passage between the north end of the Island of Bute and the mainland. Since she was sold to J. & J. Hay Ltd. in 1946 and renamed *Spartan* we know that she survived this incident.

"DAILY EXPRESS", 22nd.Novr., 1930.

"VICTOR".

'The backwash from the jetty, caused by a strong east wind, filled the hold of this steam-lighter, which sank in Dunoon harbour at high water.'

The *Victor* (built 1896) was raised and repaired but the report of the incident suggests that the hatch boards and tarpaulin had been left off in bad weather. The master deserved a severe reprimand at the very least.

However, reproduced below are some real puffer stories. All are based on fact. They must be for they are taken from newspapers of the day and other documentary evidence. The reader is invited to use his imagination and use them for the basis of an 'original' Para Handy tale. No prize is offered by the publisher but would-be authors will not find it difficult to contact any of the radio or television companies with his finished product.

The Evening Citizen, Boxing Day 1894

'At Glasgow Marine Policy Court today – Bailie Burt on the bench – John Steel, master of the steam lighter *Celt*, was charged with having on 29th Nov., while in charge of said vessel, then sailing up the river Clyde, and while passing Scotstoun shipbuilding yard in the vicinity of a launch, failed to observe signals displayed in two small boats in the river and passed one of them before the launch had taken place or the signals were withdrawn. The maximum penalty for such offence is £5 or thirty days imprisonment. He pleaded not guilty.

Robert Lust, one of the men on board the east small boat, said the *Celt* was about a mile down river when he first noticed her. There was nothing to prevent those on the *Celt* seeing the signal but she passed the Scotstoun yard while the launch, the *Evandale*, was moving. He though the *Celt* would be run down but she got past and that was all.

Bailie Burt found the charge proven and imposed a penalty of 21 shillings or 14 days imprisonment.'

Scottish Daily Mail, August 1936

'There was 30 ft. for Skipper D. C. to get his puffer *Tuscan* between the yachts as he attempted to negotiate the Crinan Canal. But the Skipper – who had been through the Canal many times in his 26 years on the puffers – had spent two hours in a hotel having a refreshment. He struck one yacht on the starboard side then scraped another on the port side.'

Evening News,
June 1952
'There is daylight in the *Moonlight*. The crew of *Moonlight*, five in number, enjoy cabins of which each has its own porthole, is lit at night by electric light and has running water laid on.

There is no cramped fo'c'sle forrard with its 'bogey' (a small black stove which provided all the heating and cooking facilities and usually belched black smoke at regular intervals) and its swinging hurricane lamp the only means of illumination where daylight seldom penetrated.'

Falkirk Herald,
January 1955
'The vessel *Starlight* from Greenock was ice-bound on the Forth and Clyde Canal at High Bonnybridge early this week. The ice-breaker *Clydeforth* was needed to break the five inch thick ice.'

Sworn under oath before a
Notary Public in Paisley,
April 1958
'I, W. W., being master of the ss *Stormlight*, owned by Ross and Marshall Ltd, hereby state that on the 11th of February 1958, a cargo of whisky in Hogsheads and Barrels was loaded in ss *Stormlight* at Port Ellen for Paisley where it was discharged. The loading was accomplished by and under the supervision of the Consignors and on completion the hold was battened down and sealed. The seal was not broken until the Stevedore at Paisley arrived to commence discharging. During the discharge it was discovered that one of the casks was leaking, work stopped and the Customs and Excise

'The heavy snowfall which transformed the West of Scotland into a fairyland yesterday made this barge on the Forth & Clyde Canal at Glasgow seem like an icebreaker.'

Hero was owned by J. & J. Hay Ltd. Built by them in their own yard in 1896 it was one of the last iron hulled lighters that they produced.

Officer was informed who in turn inspected the cask.

I hereby state, on oath, that the above particulars are true and that there was no interference with the cargo by myself or my crew and I make this solemn declaration conscientiously believing the same to be true and by virtue of the provisions of the 'Statutory Declaration Act of 1875.

sgn

W.S. Master'

'I, A. A., being employed by Archibald Young (Paisley) Ltd as manager, hereby

Crewmen are seen here loading/stowing casks of whisky from Coal Isla distillery on Islay. (D. MacDonald Collection)

state that on 14th February 1958 a cargo of whisky was discharged ex ss *Stormlight* at Paisley Harbour. The cargo was accomplished by and under the supervision of myself. During discharge it was found that one (1) cask was damaged and this was reported to the Roseburn Bonding Co Ltd. A Customs Officer was in attendance, also a cooper sent by the aforementioned Bond who repaired the cask. There was no further damage seen by me.

I hereby state on oath that the above particulars are true and that there was no interference of the cargo by myself or my dockers and I make this solemn declaration conscientiously believing the same to be true by virtue of the provisions of 'The Statutory Declaration Act of 1875.'

sgn

A.A.'

The Glasgow Herald, **June 1965**
'Flash of Inspiration'

Recently Ross and Marshall acquired a coaster and as well as changing her name to *Polarlight* they wanted her colours changed to their own livery.

A painter in the docks at Hull was told what the funnel should look like – from the top, black white, black and red. Just to make sure he got it right the new owners gave him a book of matches advertising the firm with a picture of a Ross and Marshall funnel. So faithfully did the painter follow this model that the *Polarlight* (for a time) sailed the seas with a black, white, black red funnel – and a most artistic white highlight running from top to bottom.'

One of the distinguishing features of both *Pibroch*s was the White Horse emblem at her masthead, an early example of brand advertising. A member of the crew is descending the mast having washed and combed the animal or perhaps having collected some fertiliser for the Master's roses. (D. MacDonald Collection)

Working for the Post Office. The lighters were frequently chartered by the General Post Office for cable laying activities in the Highlands and Islands. *Glenaray* is seen here with the cable, which would be coiled in her hold, trailing aft through a block suspended from her derrick.

Of Coal, Whisky and Seaweed

The Ross and Marshall ships' diaries going back to 1880 have survived and it is possible to spend many hours poring over them if you are a dedicated shipping buff, determined to get a detailed picture of the day to day movements of the lighters over a century ago. Appendix VI shows the diaries of SS *Starlight* of 1880, MV *Raylight* of 1963 and another *Starlight*, two generations later, also of 1963.

When comparison is made between the pattern of trading of two inside boats across a period of eighty years there is remarkably little difference. The 1963 *Starlight* was a direct descendant of her 1880 predecessor being a typical steam driven 120 tonner. The Clyde and its inner firth is common to the logs of both for the month of March with occasional excursions to Girvan, upper Loch Fyne or the fleshpots of Port Dundas, thrown in for variety. Closer analysis of the records reveals more about the economics of lighter operations. In the trade, a ship was considered to be 'working' when on passage to a loading or discharging port and when actually engaged in handling cargo. In 1880 *Starlight* worked for 24 of March's 31 days and thereby achieved a utilisation of 77%. There were no cargoes available for her for a period of 4 days (13%) and she spent 3 Sundays in enforced idleness i.e. in observing the Sabbath. In the Scotland of 1880 nobody would even have considered loading or discharging a ship on a Sunday, on religious grounds. In 1963 the utilisation was only 71% but then, apart from no work being on hand (16%), the vessel was stormbound for 3% of the time. The West Coast of Scotland is an unfriendly place in a gale with lee shores in all directions. A small unballasted ship with a top speed of 6 to 8 knots is better to remain at a quay than to consume fuel and put itself and its crew at hazard in 30 knots of wind.

In 1963 *Starlight* was on passage on one Sunday and while she was considered to be working by 'Head Office', she was not under the eagle eye of the Kirk and neither crew nor shore squads were noticeably involved in what could technically or biblically be described as labour. Not even the conventions of Victorian Scotland, which still held sway to an extent in 1963, and still hold fast in some parts of the Outer Hebrides today, insisted that a ship on passage should drop anchor at midnight on a Saturday, wherever she was, and remain there until a second after midnight on Monday morning. Nevertheless there is on record an instance of a neaped ship being left on a beach without assistance for twenty-four hours because she could be viewed from the church on the hill. It was too far away to see which men might have been involved in dragging her back to the water, but the horses would certainly have been identified, even from that distance.

In 1963 the 200 ton *Raylight* suffered a similar level of weather delay (3%) but had plenty of work to keep her occupied. The pattern of trade is very different from that of the *Starlight* with trips round the Mull of Kintyre to Islay and Gigha. The quick shift to Belfast from Gigha to load scrap steel for Glasgow can be considered as a 'return' cargo while there is no question that the whisky out of Bruichladdich was a dream for the pufferman in more ways than one. In the month she achieved 84% utilisation, an above average performance.

Certainly Glenlight targeted an average performance of 75% on 365 days/year over its entire fleet. In other words, in any hundred days a coaster could be expected to lose twenty-five operating days for gales anywhere on the coast, Sundays on certain islands, planned engineering downtime (classification society surveys etc), unplanned engineering downtime (breakdowns), lack of work and crew holidays.

The first two were considered to be Acts of God. The rest were blamed on the less than God-like staff in 'Head Office'. A ship still incurs expense when tied to a quay wall or in a dry-dock and the fact that a hundred day's costs needed to be recovered in seventy-five days of operating had to be, and was, reflected in the freights charged.

In that month in 1963 *Starlight* completed eight cargoes, carried about 960 tons and earned £630. By comparison *Raylight* carried much the same tonnage in five cargoes, earned £1200 and might have earned over £1500 had the weather not delayed the load for Colonsay. *Starlight* was a twenty-five year old steamer and, against her historical depreciation charges, looked as if she was making a contribution to company profits. *Raylight* was a new diesel-engined ship with two-thirds more cargo capacity and was decidedly repaying the investment in her. Had *Starlight* been able to complete the *Raylight* schedule her earnings would only have increased by about £100 because of her limited deadweight.

Starlight had cost about £4,000 in 1936. *Raylight* cost £54,000 in 1962 for 200 tons deadweight capacity. It is difficult to imagine that a direct replacement for *Starlight* would have cost significantly less. Certainly their costs would not have been in proportion to their relative carrying capacities. There was the rub for the small company and the skipper/owner. They were not generating enough cash flow from their operations in the 1950s to contemplate seriously replacing their Second World War tonnage with modern coasters. They had renewed their fleets by purchasing VICs from the Admiralty for about £4,000 each but these were fifteen to twenty years old, steam-driven and obsolete by the late 1950s. It was only Ross and Marshall and Hay-Hamilton that could re-invest upwards of £50,000 in

a new ship and so the smaller owners gradually faded from the scene. Going into the Hitler War there were nearly sixty ships in the West Coast trade belonging to nineteen owners. By 1966 this had fallen to twenty ships and five owners through a process of attrition and amalgamation (see Appendix VIII) The future shareholders of Glenlight dominated the scene and owned 90% of the tonnage.

These three companies had their 'own' islands to which they traditionally traded through business contacts built up over many years. Ross and Marshall, having a coal merchanting subsidiary, dealt with the coal suppliers on Jura, Islay and Skye, where they also owned a Portree company. The Hamiltons concentrated on the Outer Hebrides and Hays' ships were frequently found at Mull, Coll and Tiree. (The Clyde estuary was open to all.) Having said that there was a great deal of cross-hiring as owners chartered each others ships to meet cargo delivery demands that their own fleet programmes could not satisfy. Paisley was regarded as a Ross and Marshall port. The three mile passage up the White Cart could be accomplished only at high water and required the road bridge at Inchinan to be raised .

Of equal importance was the fact that the deadweight capacity of the total fleet had fallen to roughly half its pre-war level by 1966 (see Appendix VIII). The ships were larger and more efficient but the decline also indicated a contraction in the trade. This was certainly influenced by the relative depopulation of the Highlands and Islands. In the same period the number of people living in the area had fallen by some 15%. Indeed it is estimated that the population fell from 420,000 in 1850 to 308,000 in 1961. We know that the Forth & Clyde Canal had closed by this time and there was no doubt that competition from road transport made its presence felt generally. By the 1960s the

Glenshira at Lochmaddy pier unloading the tractor tracks of some piece of construction equipment. She was fitted with a five ton lifting capability. At the time this passed for a heavy lift capacity for a West Coaster.

Clyde estuary islands were still served by the coaster fleet but the mainland Clydeside ports were seldom supplied by sea from Glasgow.

A fragment from Hays' Lighter List (a daily diary of vessel positions) for 1952 has survived (see below). It shows where their ships were on one August day. Thirty percent of the fleet was out of action with four laid up at Kirkintilloch and another

The Lighter List for J. & J. Hay for 15th August 1952. These lists were produced every day in the puffer companies to show the position of each ship in the fleet and they were used as an aid to forward planning of their schedule. The name written beside each vessel is that of the skipper and the script is that of Jack Hay, the last managing director of J. & J. Hay. The other side of the piece of paper has on it a handwritten note from Jack Hay to the author dated some twenty years later. It was filed and that is why this unique glimpse of the state of play on one day in 1952 has survived.

LIGHTERS LIST.

Friday 15th August 1952.

GREEK	Coaling Clyde Trust Barges.
TROJAN	Coaling Clyde Trust Barges.
CELT	At Kirkintilloch.
TURK	At Kirkintilloch.
SLAV	At Kirkintilloch.
GAEL	At Dunoon discharging coal from Glasgow.
CUBAN	At Kirkintilloch Slip for overhaul.
TEXAN	At Troon loading coal for Kirn.
INCA	At Loch Striven discharging stones from Bowling.
CRETAN	At Rothesay discharging empty barrels from Irvine.
BOER	At Kirkintilloch.
CHINDIT	At Millers Bridge discharging coal from Troon.
DRUID	On Hire with B.B.E.Ltd., (loading at Princes Dock)
MOOR	At Rothesay Dock discharging limestone from Carnlough.
SERB	On way to Campbeltown with bricks from Glasgow.
TUSCAN	At Ardvasar loading stones for Rothesay Dock.
ANZAC	On Hire at s.s. "LASSELLS" at Cloughey Bay.
LASCAR	On Hire Irvine to Loch Riddon.
KAFFIR	On Kirkintilloch Slip for overhaul.
SPARTAN	On Hire towing barge Helensburgh to Invergarry.
ZULU	
DANE	At Rothesay discharging coal from Glasgow.

---

two under overhaul. Four ships were or had been outside the Clyde to Northern Ireland and the Caledonian Canal. Even then, there was no Forth & Clyde work on that particular day. The other ten were variously disposed around the Clyde estuary and it is not difficult to see how vulnerable the trade was to changes in transport methods. The coaling of the barges of the Clyde Navigation Trust disappeared when they went over to diesel propulsion. Half the cargoes in transit were coal and to destinations like Kirn and Dunoon which were increasingly accessible by road. This could also be said of Campbeltown and Miller's Bridge on the Crinan. It is not surprising that in little more than a decade Hays' fleet had been reduced to four vessels.

There is little hard evidence to indicate what were the total tonnages that the lighter fleets carried annually, or in what years they reached a peak. We do know that in the mid-1960s Ross and Marshall and Hay-Hamilton carried some 200,000 tons annually. Coal (30% of the total), roadstone and building materials were the principal cargoes.

Appendix VII gives some indication of the range of materials transported by the coasters in the 1940s. Many of them made for poor bulk cargoes and movement by sea was therefore expensive. Eventually the lorry would come to offer a cheaper and more convenient, door to door service in many cases, as the road network to remote parts of the mainland was upgraded. At this time nearly 80% of the tonnage moved by the coasters was coal. One problem was shared by road and sea transport alike when servicing the Highlands; the lack of a return load from many of the destinations.

The lightship southbound passage was a feature of the trade and an insidious additional cost in supplying the Highlands and Islands. Fitting in a cargo to bring a ship back to Ayr, Troon or Glasgow brought a rare smile to the normally troubled counte-

nance of the ship manager. If he organised the delivery of coal from the Clyde to Portree, followed by a quick shift to Broadford for a shipment of Skye marble south to the Mersey and then pushed the boat across the Irish Sea to pick up road salt from Kilroot for Campbeltown and thence back to Ayr for more coal, he became insufferably cheerful and given to sitting motionless at his desk with a far away look in his eyes.

Traditionally, sand had been the main southbound cargo. As far back as 1907 Ross and Marshall had obtained sand dredging rights from the Crown Commissioners for Lochs Etive, Sunart and Linnhe. This was often brought back to Glasgow to improve the traction of tram car wheels on rails in icy conditions but it was not always good enough for concrete making. The shell sand from the cockle strand at Barra was favoured for decorative purposes for a period and diorite (Aluminium silicate) from Staffin and slate from Easdale and Ballachulish also enjoyed

The *Turk* and the *Slav* were built in 1932 and 1929 respectively by Hay for their own use and they ended their working life coaling the dredgers and hopper barges of the Clyde Navigation Trust. The coal on the Turk should be trimmed before venturing out into the waters of the Firth. The duck boards have been extended to the rails in both cases to give the helmsman a walkway to allow him to see round the corner of the engine room casing when using the tiller. He has no protection from heat, cold or wet but he has a makeshift raised handrail to prevent him falling overboard when he has the tiller hard over! (D. MacDonald Collection)

a certain demand in the south until new materials and changing circumstances pushed them into the background. There was always a little timber available, often floated out to the ships for loading, but it was not until the post-World War II plantings of the Forestry Commission began to mature in the 1980s that the tonnages became significant.

One major exception to the dearth of export cargoes was seaweed. For possibly hundreds of years (and certainly from the mid-18th century) kelp had been burned on the islands and the ashes gathered up

Hamilton's *Rivercloy* is seen here dredging sand and passing it through a screen to separate out oversize material. Dredging rights for sand could be purchased from the Crown Commissioners and it made a useful return cargo from the islands.

and sent south in bags for the extraction of iodine. In 1946 Alginate Industries gave new impetus to the seaweed business by setting up processing plants at Barcaldine in Argyll and Girvan in Ayrshire and collection stations in the Uists at Sponish and Lochboisdale. Of the two types of seaweed processed, 'the tangle of the Isles', was washed ashore on western beaches and the stalks were removed and dried before shipment while the second, the 'brown berries', was cut at low water and roped together for the incoming tide to float off ready for towing to an assembly point. After milling in the south the alginic acids were extracted and found their way into many industrial products. That the froth on his beer was put there as the result of his own labours gave the pufferman an extra motive for slaking his thirst. At one time in the 1960s the southbound movement of dried and wet weed was entirely dependent on the

Opposite: Once at Custom House Quay puffers would often discharge sand (there appear to be mounds of sand on the quay), for Glasgow Corporation's Transport Department and perhaps load coal for Cowal, Bute or the towns of the lower Firth of Clyde. *Ardfern*, built by McGregor at Kirkintilloch in 1910, and owned at this time by Warnock of Paisley, is seen here with St Andrew's Cathedral in the background. (D. MacDonald Collection)

coaster. The interdependence between crofter and seaman was strong in this trade. Northbound freights were lower because the exported weed also earned vital income for the ship.

The second exception to the no-return-cargo rule was whisky, the major export of the island of Islay. Unique among the Hebridean islands for many reasons, not only did its population need domestic coal, building materials and fertilisers, its eight distilleries needed coal, malt and empty wooden casks. These the coaster compa-

nies were happy to transport. They were even happier to take its famous malt whiskies on the first part of their journey to the world's markets. The famous White Horse, emblem of Whyte and Mackay, was proudly carried atop the mast of the *Pibroch*, the only lighter to be owned by a distillery. But in addition to her owner's needs, she could not keep the island adequately supplied with the basic commodities of life. Both Ross and Marshall and Hamilton, in particular, were heavily involved in the Islay trade. In 1967

nearly 40% of the total tonnage carried by the two major fleets was to and from Islay and four-fifths of that was distillery traffic, including over one million gallons of whisky. Islay was the jewel in the coasting trade's crown.

In the mid-1960s the lighter trade was mostly to the West Highlands with occasional forays to the Mersey, Isle of Man, Northern Ireland's east coast and even occasionally to Orkney and Shetland. Trans-shipment employment was available from the Royal Navy in the Clyde, from the United States Navy in the Holy Loch and from the last of the transatlantic passenger liners. There was optimism that the new Highland Development Board would succeed in stimulating island economies. Caledonian-Macbrayne, with its mainly passenger and mail services, was regarded as complementary to the coaster bulk trade rather than competing with it. Dutch skipper/owners occasionally appeared on the scene with low freights and malt cargoes from the east coast to disturb any complacency felt. In contrast, other Scottish ship owners, recognising the special nature of the West Coast tended to pass the smaller cargoes offered to them to the lighters and content themselves with a small commission. The outlook at this stage was not at all discouraging for the owners. If the market for their services was unlikely to grow it was at least considered to be stable and able to produce profits if addressed professionally and efficiently.

However in 1966, a strange looking craft appeared out of the East heading towards Islay. She was owned by Eilean Sea Services Ltd. She was the *Isle of Gigha*, built with the aid of a Highland Development Board loan. She was a car-ferry, a roll-on-roll-off car-ferry and could carry commercial vehicles as well as cars. She came to grief, capsizing in November that year, but she had broken the mould and demonstrated new possibilities for the future of transport to the islands. From then on the puffer trade was to be under attack from this type of vessel.

4
THE FALL

The Light in The Glens

Glenlight Shipping Limited came into existence on 1 October 1968. Each of the founding parties, Hay-Hamilton and Ross and Marshall, owned 50% of the shares, and, in the same spirit of bonding, the name of the new company was also an amalgamation. The 'glen' was taken from the naming prefix that Hay-Hamilton used for their fleet, the origins of which went back to the first Glencloy in 1895, and the 'light' came from Ross and Marshall's Light Shipping Co. suffix which had been in use since the 1840s.

The gestation period of the new infant had been protracted. It had taken over two years from the time when the Ross and Marshall directors had decided to approach their opposite numbers, optimistically looking to establish the new operation by the end of 1966, to the time when agreement was reached. The usual advantages of the economy of scale were advanced as the underlying logic of the proposed merger; improved vessel utilisation, reduction in administrative overheads, joint rather than unilateral planning of new buildings and the maintenance of profitable rates on all traffic. This last was not the least of the reasons for the merger. Despite attempts at organising a 'conference', if so grand a term can be borrowed from international shipping circles and applied to the lighters, the

suspicion was strong over the years that secret discounts on the agreed rates were being offered. It was clear that neither company could grow except at the expense of the other and that would have meant an all out freight war!

Generations of rivalry, friendly, and sometimes not so friendly, were not easily set aside when it came down to the hard bargaining. At the end of the day a compromise, seen in retrospect as unhappy, was reached on the structure of what was to become Glenlight. Initially the company owned no ships but became simply a management organisation, jointly funded, responsible for fixing cargoes and operating the vessels. The two sets of owners had not been able to agree readily on the valuations of their respective fleets. Each had been reluctant to cede majority control to the other and had sought to minimise the amount of new capital that they injected. The two managerial staffs were brought together under one roof and they soon settled down into a cohesive unit. In truth, Glenlight functioned better in the operations room than it did in the board room.

With the ownership of the two fleets remaining separate, the sixteen ships, six from R & M, eight from H-H and two from Irvine Shipping and Trading (in which R & M had a 50% interest) were chartered to Glenlight at rates pre-determined as an agreed return on the capital

Contributing to her own Downfall. Ross and Marshall's *Moonlight* at Queen's Dock Glasgow, preparing to tow a boiler to Bowmore Distillery, Islay, in 1962. A tractor was loaded on the ship to drag the twenty ton boiler up the slip at Bowmore as there were no lifting facilities on the island capable of handling this weight. Since this was to allow the distillery to switch from coal to oil burning she was not doing herself any favours. The decline in the use of coal as a fuel contributed significantly to the reduction in the number of lighters needed to service the Islands.

value of each ship. The capital value of the combined fleet was of the order of £370,000. In the early years Glenlight often showed losses in its own accounts but then the parent companies had already taken out their profit by way of the charter.

At this time the ships still kept their original liveries (see Appendix IX for details) although a new house flag, a red and pink swallow-tailed pennant with a black 'G' on a white background, flew at the head of the new company's notepaper. Eventually a unified livery evolved with the changes in vessel ownership in 1974. With a total market of around 200,000 tons to be shipped annually and 3,100 tons of deadweight capacity to carry it, all seemed set fair for an improved service and increased profitability.

However, almost immediately Glenlight had to contend with the catastrophic loss of the Islay trade. The saga of the ro-ro ferries on the west coast of Scotland was about to begin with a vengeance. As well as the birth of Glenlight, there were two other significant events in 1968. These were the arrivals of Western Ferries and of the Scottish Transport Group on the scene.

A new ro-ro ferry, *Sound of Islay*, was launched at Port Glasgow for Western Ferries (Argyll) Ltd., which had been established by the injection of new capital into Eilean Sea Services. She started operating to Islay from West Loch Tarbert, in April that year, and charged lower rates than MacBrayne. Meanwhile, the publicly owned Scottish Transport Group was set up by purchasing the Caledonian Steam Packet Co. from British Railways and merging it with MacBrayne. The shipping division was to become known as Caledonian-MacBrayne and it was given £20 million of assets to operate. Western Ferries added a second ship in 1969 and then linked Jura into their schedules by operating the reconditioned *Sound of*

Gigha between Port Askaig and Feolin. They made a modest enough profit of £14,000 that year. Hardly an adequate return on their investment but they had made their breakthrough and it was the traditional coaster trade that suffered – particularly that to the distilleries.

The battle over the Islay route between Cal-Mac and Western Ferries could be the subject of a separate book in its own right and cannot be told in detail here. Suffice to say that an offer to buy Western Ferries was made by the S.T.G. and rejected. Cal-Mac withdrew from the service at one point in 1972 and then re-entered it with a ship converted for ro-ro traffic to compete against Western Ferries, whose profits inevitably all but vanished. It was evident that Cal-Mac was losing money and Western Ferries made it clear, in 1974, that they would withdraw if Government subsidised Cal-Mac on the route, which by then had the distinction of charging the lowest rates per mile on the West Coast and indeed in the whole of Europe. In 1975 the Scottish Office gave Cal-Mac a subsidy of £2.5 million. Was it the case that, having set up the Scottish Transport Group, Government decided that it had to be defended against the possibility of losing potentially profitable routes to private enterprise and being left with only those that had no prospect of becoming viable? If so, this was a spectre that would come back to haunt the Scottish Office many times in the future.

In summary, a situation had developed where the tax-payer was losing money subsidising the Cal-Mac service, Western Ferries was getting an inadequate return on its investment and the puffers had been driven from the scene by the artificially low freight rates.

Could the coasters have competed with ferry technology in an open market? For a time and for the bulk cargoes, they could have, almost certainly. There is no

doubting, however, the convenience that containerisation offered for the finished whisky product. Containerisation, for which road transport was particularly suited, became the favoured method of onward movement of the product from Glasgow to worldwide markets. Eventually the tonnages of coal used would have declined on Islay as they did on other islands. In 1968, at the time of Glenlight's formation, her ships carried the equivalent of 74,000 tons of traffic annually for the Islay/Jura island group. Of this 58,000 tons was for the Islay distilleries. In 1973, by which time the ro-ro ferries were established, the total tonnage had fallen to 7,500 tons.

Most of this decrease had occurred in the first twelve months of Glenlight's life and clearly there were too many ships for the trade available. R.& M withdrew and sold two of their older bottoms, *Polarlight*

Here we have three contrasting methods of launching puffers. Hay-Hamilton's third *Glencloy* is seen at Scott's yard at Bowling in 1966 prior to entering the water in what is often regarded as the conventional manner; down a slipway. In 1957 Ross and Marshall's *Stormlight* was launched sideways at Northwich. This was the conventional and only way that those vessels built at Kirkintilloch by both Hay and McGregor, before the closure of the Forth & Clyde Canal, could take to the water. Hay could be accused of seeking out unusual ways to launch their ships but in this case it would be unfair. At Papendracht, Holland, where *Druid* (III) was built in 1959, the flat landscape did not allow for the normal inclined launch and so there was no alternative but to lift the vessel into the water after the usual dousing with champagne.

and *Warlight*, and laid up *Stormlight* pending her conversion from steam. Similarly, H-H disposed of *Glenshira* and *Lascar* and this reduction in cargo capacity broadly matched the lower demand. Thereafter, for the rest of the decade, the tonnages carried to and from the West Highlands fluctuated annually in the

region of 80,000 to 100,000 tons. The fleet coped adequately with this although, from time to time, tonnage was chartered-in to meet peaks in activity.

The most noticeable change in the nature of the trade at that time was the declining demand for coal cargoes and the growth in the business of shipping road salt to the local authorities in the Highlands and Islands. Given that coal deliveries in the inner Clyde firth had kept the old Hay 120 tonners fully occupied, it was clear that their days were numbered. The fleet became progressively imbalanced with too great a demand on the time of the 240 tonners and too little work for

Spartan pictured in her steamer days. She is the last survivor of the ships built by Hays at Kirkintilloch from which she emerged in 1942 as VIC 18. She became part of the fleet sold to Glenlight Shipping after the 1968 amalgamation of Ross and Marshall and Hay-Hamilton.

the ex-VICs.

Overlaying all this activity, and to an extent pushing the real puffer trade into the background during the middle and late 1970s, was the boom in concrete oil plat-form construction on the Clyde and the West Coast of Scotland. Glenlight had a roller coaster experience in this market making substantial profits in some years and losing money in others as the level of activity fluctuated. Additional tonnage was chartered, in the form of 1,500 dead-weight ships, to supply MacAlpine's yard at Ardyne Point, on the Cowal peninsula, with 10,000 tons per week of aggregates and sand for the casting of the massive concrete structures for the deep waters of the North Sea. Later a similar service was provided for Howard-Doris when the company's own 400 tonners ran materials from a quarry at Kyleakin on Skye to Loch Kishorn. It turned out to be a relatively

short-lived expansion of the traditional West Coast market but the opportunity had to be grasped while it was there.

Leaving aside the diversion into the North Sea oil industry, Glenlight was facing some critical decisions after five years of existence. Thought had to be given to the next generation of ships. The 120 tonners were practically killed off when, for example, the domestic gas supply on Bute was switched from coal to natural gas. Vessels had been lost. *Kaffir* was run aground off Ayr and *Stormlight*, commented upon earlier, stranded at Jura after an engine breakdown. *Glenshiel* sank, mysteriously, with tragic loss of life, on a night passage from Ayr to Glasgow in 1973. The fleet was thus reduced to eight ships and was struggling to meet its commitments as the major supplier of bulk shipping services to the Highlands and Islands.

Other strains were showing. The parent companies' interests were diverging. Clyde Shipping who had taken all of the original Ross and Marshall holdings into direct control was still interested in developing Glenlight and had the resources to do so. Hay-Hamilton did not wish to turn its back on its roots but the development of its other interests was taking time and money. It had made losses on its Speedcranes subsidiary and, being smaller than Clyde, had felt Glenlight's problems with the poor years in the oil industry more severely. The will was there to

Above and opposite: Glenlight Shipping bought MV *Wib* and three of her sister ships for conversion for the West Highland trading. After fitting her with a travelling gantry crane she was renamed *Glenetive*.

continue with Glenlight but Hay-Hamilton's means were distinctly scarce. It has to be said, as well, that the 50/50 split in ownership did not make for decisive action in policy-making in the board room. Eventually it was decided to break the deadlock.

In August 1974 an agreement was signed whereby the shareholding in Glenlight was restructured so that Clyde owned 62%, all the remaining ships were sold to Glenlight and additional capital was injected. Hay-Hamilton were able to take cash out of the business and were given the right to withdraw further, if they so desired, by requiring Clyde to progressively acquire their remaining shares in equal amounts over the period from 1975 to 1979.

In fact Hay-Hamilton's departure from

the scene was accelerated. Speedcranes continued to be a drain on their resources, although there were profitable years in that business. They finally sold out the last of their shares in Glenlight in September 1976 at the net asset value at that time. So came to an end a long and distinguished association with the West Highland trade of two of its oldest and most successful family companies. For at least 130 years the Hamiltons had sailed out of Arran, and certainly since 1895, they had contributed significantly to the technical advancement of the puffer. To the Hays went the distinction of being one of the most consistent and successful builders of these specialised little ships and being the owners, at their peak, of the largest fleet of steam lighters in Scotland. Both the Hays and the Hamiltons had contributed in no small measure to the prosperity of the West of Scotland and to the commonweal of the Highlands and Islands.

Before their departure, Hay-Hamilton had contributed to the debate on re-tonnaging. By 1974 the fleet stood at eight ships, with a deadweight capacity of half of the 3,000 tons it had begun with in 1968. No new ships had been built since. There was practically no work for the 120 tonners, of which there were still three, except for transhipment work for the United States Navy at the Holy Loch. Design studies for bigger versions of the 240 tonners had been commissioned in Scotland and Holland and all had indicated building prices of around £260,000 to £300,000 for a 300 ton deadweight ship capable of carrying containers and having a 30 ton crane. (The *Glencloy* had cost £56,000 in 1966.) Since two ships were needed to restore the fleet capacity the

solution was costly and, given the delivery times indicated by the yards, were two years away at least. Second hand tonnage had to be seriously considered.

A fleet of five 400 ton deadweight vessels owned by Eggar Forrester of London were identified and an approach made. Four were sister ships built in 1968–70 and in length and draft were ideally suited to the West Highland trade, especially since their gross registered tonnage was 199.9. (So there was no need to change the established crewing arrangements.) They had one major disadvantage; they were gearless. A bargain was struck to buy/charter the entire fleet as at this time the company was entering into negotia-

tions with Howard-Doris to supply sand and aggregate to their Loch Kishorn construction yard. Speedcranes, the Hay-Hamilton subsidiary, designed gantry cranes which could travel on rails along the length of the hatch coamings and after protracted negotiations with the Highlands and Islands Development Board loans were made available to purchase them. As a result of retro-fitting these to the ships the cargo capacity was reduced to about 340 tons deadweight but this still offered the advantage of carrying a third more than the *Glencloy* class with the same crew and much the same bunker consumption. The ships were also capable of taking containers on deck and had 240 tons ballast available in their double bottoms. As a class of ship they had distinct advantages for the trade.

The deal was signed in June 1975 and the purchase of the ships was completed in 1977. The price was £690,000 without the subsequent cost of the cranes and was, at that time, the biggest single investment in the future of the coaster trade made by any company. They were not new but it was in effect five for the price of two new-buildings. Four of them came into West Highland service progressively from early 1978 onwards as the traffic at Loch Kishorn came to a close. Two were named 'glens'; Etive and Rosa and two 'lights'; Sea and Polar and so the naming traditions were continued.

Since they were capable of carrying 100 tons more than the 240 ton class, efforts were made to persuade cargo consignees to trade up in their delivered weights to take advantage of the economies of scale. (It is not the cost of transporting commodities to the Islands that puts them at an economic disadvantage. It is the small size of the parcels that are required to satisfy local needs that puts the unit cost up to higher levels than on the mainland.) This was only partially successful; there are practical limits to how much coal a merchant can reasonably be expected to take. However, subdividing the hold with moveable bulkheads allowed the ships to carry up to three, 100-ton parcels for three different destinations on a single voyage and in this way some of the benefits of scale were achieved.

As the company went into 1979 the portents were not at all bad. The oil platform construction flurry had come and gone and the West Highland trade had settled at around 80/90,000 tons per annum. The fleet was renewed and was capable of servicing its customers more effectively with fewer bottoms; the older smaller ships were being sold. There were encouraging signs that timber movement south from the Highlands and Islands was going to be the growth cargo of the future. So much so that the crane for the third 400 tonner to come into service was to be designed with an hydraulic grab to handle sawn logs. Glenlight faced its second decade positively, having come through a difficult period of change of ownership and fleet re-organisation. The mood of optimism was dispelled by an attack from an unexpected quarter.

The Scottish Transport Group stole the seaweed trade.

There was some 6,000 tons of badly-needed southbound cargo and over £40,000 of income at stake. The business was being taken away because the coasters' freight rate was being undercut by the highly subsidised public utility group. Glenlight could not take that lying down.

The Vital Subsidy
(Mrs MacArthur's Coal)

The seaweed for Alginate Industries was southbound from the Uists and Harris and was inextricably linked to the northbound movement of coal for the same customers. The effect of losing the business was therefore twofold on Glenlight.

For the movement of the dried weed from Harris there were two lorry and ferry alternatives offered by the Scottish Transport Group. One was by road north to Stornaway, ferry to Ullapool and road south to Barcaldine (130 miles) or all the way to the Girvan factory (250 miles). The other, the Uig triangle ferry route, meant travelling by road to Lochmaddy, ferry to Uig on Skye, road down through Skye to Kyleakin, ferry to Kyle of Lochalsh and road journeys of again between 130 and 250 miles to the two southern destinations. How could either of these two ferry routes compete with the direct coaster passages from port to port? Quite simply; the road vehicles and the ferries were owned by the same subsidised public utility and since its lorries were returning empty from the islands and not otherwise earning anything, the notion of loading them with seaweed at a small charge for the lorry and the ferry had the effect of increasing income. In other words the commercial rate was undercut. The S.T.G.'s overall operating cost was offset by this new source of revenue. From the perspective of the combined road haulage and sea transport organisation it made perfect sense.

Not surprisingly the commercial organisation cried foul. What right had the S.T.G. to use a subsidy to compete unfairly with Glenlight or anyone else for that matter? As an alternative transport method the lorry/ferry mode did not remotely begin to address the criterion of the most effective use of resources. Not for the last time on the west coast, private enterprise and nationalised transport were thrown into conflict.

Glenlight took its case to the Chairman of the Highlands and Islands Development Board and to the Scottish Development Department (S.D.D.). Both saw the problem and both saw the logic of Glenlight's argument. What was Government policy to be? Was Glenlight to leave the stage clear for the ferries to be the sole supplier of shipping services? Since it was obvious that the coasters could supply a type of service that the ferries could not, there was no intention to drive them from the seas. So what was the policy on competition to be if one was subsidised and the other was not? Answer: If both are given support in an appropriate way then they could establish commercial rates and the islander would be free to choose on the basis of service and price.

A mechanism for enabling support for the coasters already existed in the form of the Highlands and Islands Shipping Services Act of 1960. Its general purpose was to provide a means of ameliorating the cost of transporting commodities to the remote communities of the North. It was then being used, for example, to provide discounts to the islanders of Orkney and Shetland on the import and export of goods and livestock. The system used was known as the Tariff Rebate Subsidy Scheme or T.R.S. And so Glenlight started down the primrose path of seeking the 'Vital Subsidy'.

Basically the T.R.S. system allowed the recipient of a cargo to claim a discount on the freight charged by the shipping company that delivered his goods. For example, if the freight for taking a ton of fertiliser to Mull was £10, the islander was given a discount of, say, 30% and was therefore asked to pay only £7, i.e. the £10 less the £3 discount. A copy of the shipping invoice was passed to the S.D.D. who

Here *Glenshiel* is shooting the rapids under Connel Bridge at Loch Etive. The notorious currents here are caused by a ridge of uneven rock in the sea bed that runs two-thirds of the way across the channel. This ship was lost in 1973 while on a night passage from Ayr to Glasgow to pick up deck cargo. The wreck was found on the sea bed near the Lady Isle, off Ayr, and all but one of her complement were drowned. The subsequent enquiry put the responsibility on the shifting of coal cargo and the failure of the master to fit the hatch tarpaulin. Many, including the author, felt that this was an unsatisfactory answer to the question of why she was lost.

gave the shipper the 'missing' £3. The islander got his cargo less expensively, the ship owner got his full freight and the Government of the day got the credit for having an enlightened approach to the problems of Scotland's remote communities. (See Appendix X for the full calculation.)

At that time different rates applied for northbound and southbound traffic to the Northern Isles and Glenlight's debate with the S.D.D. centred round the question of with what level of discount T.R.S. should apply to the Western Isles. The civil servants suggested a flat rate of 30%, which had the virtue of simplicity of administration, but Glenlight sought to have the problem of the truly social services, the small cargoes to the small islands, addressed by having different rates of T.R.S. used for different island groupings.

Common usage has not coined a phrase for the converse of the 'economy of scale' but whatever that might be it could be used justifiably to describe commercial activity in the West Highlands. The passage time for a ship from Ayr to Portree is exactly the same as that to Raasay, barely one mile to the east of Skye's capital. The cost of operating a ship to carry 400 tons of coal to Portree was much the same as to take 100 tons to Raasay. Portree's demand for coal came to several 400 ton shipments a year but 100 tons for the smaller island was the total coal consumption for the entire population for a whole year. The cost per ton to the shipowner for delivering coal to Raasay was actually four times that of taking it to Skye. He should have charged the good people of Raasay quadruple the rate that he got from the equally good people of Portree in order to recover his expenses!

Rather than place this intolerable burden on the Raasay islanders the shipper took account of the fact that he got an adequate rate for the Skye business and charged the same freight for both islands. But this happy logic broke down when other parties came on the scene and started to 'cherry pick' the attractive business, like the southbound seaweed, and leave the established shipper with only the loss makers. The reality was that if both routes were to be equally profitable to Glenlight then the Raasay freight ought to be have been higher and the Government discount to have been sufficient to adjust the delivered price to the same level for both islands. It was clearly going to be difficult to present such a complex argument publicly without a high risk of being misunderstood. A single rate of 30%, to be applied without distinction as to cargo destination, was favoured by the S.D.D. despite the fact that Glenlight considered there were arguments for a rate of 50% (see Appendix X).

The tariff rebate went of course to the cargo consignee and not to the shipowner so what was in it for the shipper? Well, frankly nothing unless – unless it meant that he could charge a commercial rate that would show him a profit. If profitable trading necessitated putting the freight rates up then the Tariff Rebate Subsidy Scheme could be used to ameliorate the cost to the islander by giving a correspondingly high rebate. If not, why should the coaster owner continue to supply a loss making service to these smaller communities? The S.D.D. preferred to keep the rebate at 30% rather than set it at the 50% that was really needed but recognised the 'Raasay problem' and proposed a subvention for any proven deficit incurred on such West Highland routes. This was not an open-ended commitment and was subject to rigorous independent audit. Glenlight had to meet pre-determined standards of operating efficiency and the S.D.D. had the right to claw back any promised deficit funding. So instead of

The bucket discharge was the traditional method of unloading for the coal clubs. These co-operatives were formed by small communities to buy coal cargoes and organise their shipment. Payment was for each bucket-full delivered to each house by cart or lorry. It was hard work filling the buckets by shovel. Since there are eleven men on view we may take it that the crew were being helped by local men.

getting the higher discount system Glenlight was offered, and accepted, the lower rate and a cash sum.

The negotiations between Glenlight and the S.D.D. in order to reach this agreement had taken most of 1979 and the company was anxious to put the new arrangement into place as quickly as possible, preferably for the fiscal year beginning in April 1980. Parliamentary time had to be found to put these agreements into effect as the House of Commons had to approve the Secretary of State for Scotland entering into an agreement with Glenlight in terms of the Highland Shipping Act. The critical date came and went with the draft undertaking being processed somewhere in the depths

of the legal department of the Scottish Office. There was, of course, no possibility of making the agreement retro-active. When nothing had happened by October 1980, Glenlight requested and was given a meeting with the Minister who was far from encouraging that the Government could actually proceed at all. Public support for Glenlight was forthcoming from Scottish MPs and it was explained that if the undertaking was not put in place the company would have to withdraw some of its services. The delays may have been designed to test the company's resolve. It rose to the implied challenge but it might not have succeeded without the assistance of a redoubtable Highland lady, Mrs MacArthur.

A feature of the puffer trade was that coal clubs were among its most important customers. A coal club was perhaps an uniquely West Highland institution, wherein a crofting community would unite in organising the shipment of a cargo of coal from the south. Individual requirements would be ascertained and aggregated and a suitable time for a delivery would be agreed. When the secretary of the club, a position of some status in the community, judged that there was sufficient demand for it (a hundred tons or so) the purchase and shipment of a cargo was organised. The cost per ton was calculated and the money collected for the actual weight of coal delivered to each front door. The cargo was not discharged by ship's grab but by 'buckets', filled by shovel by the ship's crew, and loaded into whatever receptacle, trailer or cart, that the individual homestead possessed. Traditionally each bucket held a ton, and if it did not actually do so it was the accepted measure. Mrs. MacArthur had the organising of a cargo of coal for Strontian, on Loch Sunart, for delivery in 1980. In the face of what it saw as Government intransigence, Glenlight announced that, in the circumstances, it was unable to deliver the cargo. Mrs. MacArthur was a trifle upset by this turn of events.

Strontian typifies many small mainland highland communities. It lies in the north of Argyll and can only be approached by ferry across Loch Linnhe and a single track road from Fort William or by sea from Loch Sunart. In 1980 this latter route was the only sensible one for a bulk cargo. (Strontian is famous as the place whose lead mines yielded the mineral from which the element Strontium was first extracted.) It was November and it was cold. Strontian's coal supplies were running low and its Member of Parliament belonged to the party of the Government. That MP was probably the first to receive Mrs. MacArthur's strongly held and pithily expressed views on the importance of coastal shipping to the well- being of the Highlands.

The promise of a space in the Parliamentary timetable was made. The coal was shipped to Strontian. The Undertaking was debated in the House of Commons on January 19th 1981 and passed without dissent.

It is worth noting what *Hansard* reported that the Minister said on this occasion, for it was to become a central point in future discussions between Glenlight and the S.D.D. He recognised the vital role played by Glenlight and the problem of servicing the smallest communities at an acceptable cost to them and at an acceptable price to the shipper. 'Increased freight charges... would be so great and have to be unevenly applied between the islands as to produce a transport cost which we would consider unbearable by the largely very remote communities served by the company. The Secretary of State proposes a combination of a short term contribution towards any trading deficit made on the company's Highlands and Islands services and percentage rebate on its tariffs. *In addition the system is designed to allow the phasing out of the deficit subsidy with a measure of Government assistance being shifted annually from the contribution to deficit to further percentage reduction in rates.*' (The italics are added for emphasis.)

Henceforth Glenlight's trading would be divided into Highland (H.I.D.B.) and non-Highland, for the writ of the Shipping Act did not run outside the H.I.D.B. area. Thus the traditional work to Ireland, the Isle of Man and even the islands of the inner Firth of Clyde did not qualify for either T.R.S. or deficit subsidy, because by definition they did not come under the aegis of the Highlands and Islands Development Board.

The arrangement came into effect in April 1981 with a T.R.S. rate of 25% and an offer of a maximum deficit grant of £80,000 which was to depend on the actual operating loss on the cargoes to which T.R.S. applied. An important additional provision of the Undertaking was that Glenlight could receive capital grants for the acquisition of facilities to improve services. It was a very significant step forward in regularising Glenlight's status as the primary shipper of bulk cargoes to the Highlands and Islands. But the company never did recapture the seaweed trade.

Given this position of relative security the company moved into a period of modest development and expansion over the next few years. Appendix XI shows the profits made from 1979 to 1987, the next year of significance in the saga of the subsidy. They look healthy enough but, these profits and the depreciation of the historical values of the ships, did not quite generate enough cash flow to support re-investment for the future. As can be seen, the H.I.D.B. trade was not profitable without the deficit grant and even after that it was not as rewarding to the company as other parts of its business. This was gently pointed out to the Scottish Office and in late 1982, at their request, Glenlight put forward a detailed planning document on the future of shipping services to the H.I.D.B. area. This proposed, inter alia, that a return on capital invested should be built into the financial support given to any company providing lifeline services. It was also suggested that shipping services should be licensed by Government and put out to competitive tender and that the next generation of puffers should be designed to play a complementary role to the ferries, for example, to alleviate their burden in the periods of high tourist activity. This was in fact a plea for an integrated transport policy for the Highlands.

The last two points were well received but not acted upon. The first was rejected although it was pointed out that the return on capital element was built into the company's contract with the United States Navy at the Holy Loch. The Americans had little problem with the concept, believing that their suppliers had to be profitable to be able to continue to give the service. The idea found favour in the Land of the Free but curiously not in the Land of the Enterprise Culture.

In this period the 400 tonners became fully operational on the West Coast with the final two vessels being fitted with hydraulic grabs for timber handling. Logs from Kilmichael forest in Kintyre had been successfully moved from Ardrishaig to Girvan in September 1980 although the first time Glenlight loaded a full cargo of timber from a Highland pier had been from Lochaline a few months earlier. The tonnage of wood shipped grew throughout the decade and did much to compensate for the decline in coal movements, which as far as Glenlight, was concerned did not recover from the 1984 coal strike. (The company was given dispensation by both the coal management and unions to break the strike and to carry essential supplies to the islands. The definition of essential was flexible enough to include 100 tons for the Bunnahabhain distillery.) In 1980 Glenlight carried 16,000 tons of domestic coal to the islands and brought back virtually no timber at all. Six years later it was carrying 16,000 tons of logs south for the paper and board manufacturers and only 6,000 tons of coal northwards, although increasing demand for road salt was filling the gap. Broadly speaking in this period, roughly half of Glenlight's turnover was earned in the H.I.D.B. jurisdiction with the rest split between traditional non-T.R.S. work and the United States Navy (see Appendix XII).

The demand for timber was expected to grow to 30,000 tons per annum and serious consideration had to be given to the configuration of the fleet, the backbone of which was now the ageing 400 tonners. All the smaller ships were sold or laid up and one of the last 240 tonners was on full time charter for the lighterage work for the U.S. Navy. Debate centred on the advisability of buying a 600 tonner, a size previously thought too large for most West Highland ports and cargo demands. However this size did offer advantages for the important and bulky commodities such as road salt and logs.

The S.D.D. was asked to contribute capital to this project, as the Undertaking gave it the power to do, but it had put a moratorium on capital spending for both Glenlight and Cal-Mac while it commissioned and considered an independent study of the shipping needs of the Southern Hebridean islands. (It was a time of much discussion about the future shape of West Highland shipping services and many papers were exchanged between the Scottish Office and interested parties. The idea of privatising Cal-Mac was also given one of its airings.) The outcome was not satisfactory for Glenlight as its request for support was denied. Indeed the company was not ever, at any time, to receive capital assistance from the Scottish Office for its Highland and Island services. However it went ahead with the project and by June 1986 a second-hand 600 tonner, renamed *Glencloy*, was on station, fitted out with a gantry crane for handling bulk commodities and timber.

This year was to be a watershed in the life of Glenlight. It took two body-blows. The U.S. Navy changed its pattern of operations at the Holy Loch and substantially reduced its need for trans-shipments. A reduced service was provided for several more years but the company suffered a substantial drop in turnover from this source. More significant was the statement by the S.D.D. that it intended to cease paying the deficit funding for the H.I.D.B. services. This was regarded as a major breach of faith.

The conditions for the operation of the T.R.S. had been negotiated annually and modified as considered appropriate between the company and the S.D.D. Latterly the civil servants had argued, and Glenlight had agreed, that it should not increase its freights above the rate of inflation and consequently there was no need to adjust the T.R.S. percentage upwards either. This had had the effect of putting the plan, put forward by the Government in the House of Commons in 1981, gradually to reduce the deficit grant by increasing the level of the T.R.S., on hold.

T.R.S. had not been progressively increased which would have compensated for a step-by-step removal of the deficit payment and now the Government was declaring its intention to stop this subsidy completely.

The Seven Year War

The fact that Glenlight had an undertaking with the Scottish Office was not popular with other shippers who were engaged in the West Highland trade to a lesser or greater extent. In 1982 others were given Undertakings by the S.D.D. to allow them to apply T.R.S. to their freights on cargoes bound for the H.I.D.B. area. However none of them was given the right to receive either deficit grants or assistance with capital investment. This rankled in some quarters. It was not any part of Glenlight's case that others should not have equal rights with it and it said so on many occasions. Sadly, and negatively, some shippers concentrated on attacking Glenlight's 'unfair advantage' rather than

The last *Glencloy* is seen here discharging at the foot of Neptune's Staircase on the Caledonian Canal with Ben Nevis in the background.

seeking parity. Such a debate could have made the Government face the question of what the policy on bulk shipments to the area was to be. Lack of it did no-one any good and certainly worked to the disadvantage of the trade to the Highlands and Islands as a whole.

Be that as it may, S.D.D. announced that deficit support was to cease at the end of March 1987, i.e. within three months of the end of Glenlight's 1986 financial year. The effect of the policy of freezing freight rates at the request of the S.D.D. and thus of not increasing the T.R.S. rate meant that Glenlight's trading to the H.I.D.B. area in the 1980s had stayed loss making if it had not been for the deficit payment, as Appendix X shows. Yet, given normal commercial freedom to negotiate freight rates, the company had made profits in its traditional non-H.I.D.B. business, which for decades had been as much part of the puffer trade as the artificially demarcated

administrative area to which the 1960 Act applied. The problem was that Glenlight was spending half its operating time and earning half its income from the H.I.D.B. area and would get no return for it without the subsidy. Under the injunction of the S.D.D. half of the company's resources would become unproductive and drag down the rest of the company.

The rest of 1986 and much of 1987 was taken up with representations to the S.D.D. and to Government ministers. The deadline for the cessation of the deficit funding was extended to March 1988, the end of the S.D.D's financial year. Only £45,000 of deficit grant was paid in December 1987, which was Glenlight's financial year end, and in the H.I.D.B. area trading went into the red. In August a consultative document on the operation of the T.R.S. system was issued for public debate and comment. Government's intention was that an amended system should be introduced for April 1988. Naturally Glenlight, as the largest and most vitally concerned West Highland bulk trader, participated avidly in this process. This April 1988 deadline was not met but the deficit payment stopped promptly, even though the consultation process was incomplete. The life of the 'old' T.R.S. was extended until October.

When the result of the review was announced it could not have been more damaging to Glenlight's prospects. The intended system was much more complex than the original and was administratively cumbersome both for the S.D.D. and the user. For the first time different rates of T.R.S. were to be applied to Northbound and to Southbound cargoes. A variety of rates were to applied for different commodities. The rate for all cargoes carried to the islands was increased to 40% but all 'imports' to the mainland of the H.I.D.B. area were disqualified completely from any assistance. (This meant that a 40% discount was available on goods delivered to Kyleakin on Skye but not to Kyle of Lochalsh half a mile across the strait on the mainland!) Some commodities, like timber, were restricted to a tonnage limit after which T.R.S. would not apply. Most importantly, from Glenlight's point of view, all cargoes intended for local authorities were to be excluded from the scheme. Given that the company had contracts to take up to 30,000 tons of road salt annually from Northern Ireland to all the local authorities in the Highlands and Islands, this was a disastrous decision for it and the local authorities. Calculations showed that the new system would cost the latter £180,000 per annum in lost discounts on the freights for salt.

Cynics saw in this the fine hand of the Treasury trying to make savings on transport costs to the Highlands. The even more cynical saw the disqualification of discounts to the local authorities, in the period prior to the introduction of the Community Services Charge, popularly known as the Poll Tax, as a way of exposing these bodies to the true costs of providing their services. Glenlight was concerned that a major customer, faced with a large increase in the freight of its salt would use another transport method. What is more, the viability of the price structure of southbound cargoes depended on ships being in the north, with salt for example.

Glenlight's situation was critical. It was already having to adjust to the downturn in the United States Navy business and the loss of its deficit subsidy. As a consequence it had laid up tonnage and made staff redundant. Now its salt cargoes, accounting for around 30% of its turnover, were under threat and timber, its one cargo commodity with potential for growth, was to be limited because only

24,000 tons per annum would qualify under the T.R.S. scheme.

Some hard thinking was necessary. The Clyde Shipping Board decided to give Glenlight a year to attempt to resolve its problems one way or another. A deep breath was taken and the company sailed into battle. The first priority was to convince the S.D.D. that however elegant a rationalisation their new system appeared to them in Edinburgh it would have catastrophic effects on the West Coast. A 'Save the Puffers' campaign was considered and public relations firms were interviewed. However it was decided to keep the highly technical arguments out of the public domain though interested MPs were kept informed.

A series of meetings with S.D.D. officials were requested and granted, culminating in an interview with the Minister of State. The detailed arguments were presented but initially met with a negative response. Two letters to the Minister at the end of 1988, quoted below, summarise the company's stance at that time :

'... we have taken the decision to withdraw from providing a comprehensive service to the H.I.D.B. area. This decision we have made as a direct consequence of the proposed changes to the Tariff Reduction Scheme... There will be considerable criticism and outcry when we make it known exactly why we have been forced into this situation and it is inevitable that attention will be focused on the policies of your Department.'

'In 1987 Glenlight transported over 77,000 tons of commodities to and from forty-six Highland 'ports'. Of this total approximately 65% was Northbound. Virtually all of the Southbound cargoes were logs, carried on the return legs of Northbound loads, half of which were road salt for local authorities. We hope that it will now become clear to you why in previous correspondence to you we have talked of the revision of the T.R.S. system increasing our loss in the H.I.D.B. area by over £200,000 per annum. We urge you to reconsider the recent decisions on the restructuring of the T.R.S. system.'

(A full analysis of this 77,000 tons is given in Appendix XIII. as it provides a picture of how far, across the West Highlands the Glenlight ships were ranging even in the late 1980s.)

To be fair to the Minister he did reconsider although deficit funding was not restored which meant that Glenlight's future in the H.I.D.B. area depended entirely on getting T.R.S. at a level that both made the company profitable and kept costs stable for the islander. The Minister did fully restore T.R.S. for mainland crofters' coal clubs and a rate of 20% was allowed on salt for a six month period though subsequently reduced to 10%. The changes were a compromise but were encouraging as far as they went.

Glenlight continued to rationalise its cost structure and to develop other markets, specifically a bulk liner service to the Isle of Man to balance what was seen as a break-even situation on West Highland trading. The period of adjustment was painful and losses were incurred in 1989 which were aggravated by the sinking of *Polarlight* off the Isle of Man. (She foundered when a cargo of bulk cement shifted in heavy weather. Thankfully no lives were lost.) Considerable Board discussion centred on whether or not to replace this ship. It was a matter of invest or divest. The decision was made, based on the growth potential of the market for timber, to buy another ship.

The Forestry Commission's post-World War II plantings in remote areas of the mainland were maturing and the paper and cardboard manufacturers, notably Caledonian Paper at Irvine and Iggesund at Workington, both conveniently situated near West coast ports, were projecting large increases in their demand for such timber. Log cargoes had grown significantly in number since 1980 (see Appendix XII) and in 1989 had accounted for 35% of the company's turnover. Future profitability was seen to lie in a stabilisation of the existing business and in the growth of the timber trade. A second-hand 400 tonner was purchased, fitted with a log-handling crane and named *Glenfyne*, the original of that name having been sold in 1987.

The cautious optimism with which 1990 was approached was reinforced by two developments, both of which were interesting departures from the traditional form of West Highland bulk shipping.

The first was the shipment of bottled gas, the modern replacement for all those coal cargoes which had been the staple of the Highland coasting trade for many years. An interesting Bulk/Ro-Ro design ship was taken on charter from Norwegian owners to prove the planned multi-port delivery concept and to explore the possibility of developing that type of vessel for the future of Glenlight's general West Coast trade. By the end of the year, after intense negotiations over freight rates, the gas business went to a combination of road transport and Cal-Mac ferries (shades of the seaweed battle of ten years earlier) and the cost of the experiment was written off. The type of ship, very flexible and successful in Norwegian coastal waters, pointed the way to the evolution of a new method of servicing Scotland's remote communities by combining the best aspects of the Glenlight coaster and the Cal-Mac ferry. Such a ship could have built a bridge between the two modes of shipping and even between the two companies.

The second development came from the explosion in the demand for felled timber. Glenlight was then moving 35,000 tons per annum from West Coast forests. It was projected that this would rise to 100,000 tons by 1995 and would eventually reach 300,000 by the end of the century, if, as expected, paper-making capacity in Scotland doubled. To deal with such an increase Glenlight developed the tug-and-barge configuration for Highland waters (see Appendix XIV) and from 1992 onwards operated the coasters and the tug-and-barge in complement to each other for timber movements.

Since the 1988 compromise with S.D.D., Glenlight had continued to press for a reconsideration of the method of application of T.R.S., not only because of the anomalies introduced, but because in the 1989/90 year the S.D.D. had superimposed a new and inherently much more damaging factor; a capping of the amount of T.R.S. available. Whatever the reason, and it may have had a lot to do with the pressures to cut public spending which became a feature of Government policy in the late 1980s and early 1990s, the Scottish Office proposed to limit the amount of T.R.S. that any one company could offer its customers as discount on their transport costs.

The problem for the shipping companies posed by this proposal was potentially very serious. What was to be done with a finite amount of money? Try to spread it over all customers and then, when it ran out, remove the discount half way through the year? Be selective and give it only to some consignees and promise them that the discount could be applied all year? Faced with rising costs the shipper would have liked to put his freight rates up to make cargoes profitable but the more that was charged per ton the sooner the limited cash sum would be exhausted. (Remember that Glenlight now had no deficit payment to fall back on.) A smaller freight rate could be charged to make sure that all the tonnage could be carried before the money ran out. But Glenlight was already losing money on the Highlands and Islands trade and reducing rates would worsen this. It was a Catch 22 situation that would have brought a smile of appreciation to the lips of Mr. Joseph Heller. It was tactfully pointed out to the S.D.D. that their proposal might end up inhibiting economic activity in the Highlands, the growth of the timber business, for example. They took the point and went off to consider the position again.

While these debates went on, the underlying anomalies of the pricing structure of the West Highland trade and the normal perils of ship operating meant that 1991 was another loss making period for Glenlight. *Sealight* stranded at Lochmaddy at the end of the year and the damage to her twenty year old hull was such that she was considered to be not worth repairing. However plans were laid to charter tonnage to support the 1992 cargo demand. Everything now depended on Glenlight being able to agree a rational system of support with the Scottish Office and, of course, on bringing the tug-and-barge system into production for the increasing timber business.

The S.D.D. were unable to concede to any changes in the T.R.S. Scheme for 1992 and capped Glenlight's freight discounts at a sum of £245,000. This sum was less than the company's budget indicated would be necessary if it was to satisfy its planned cargo movements and only £5,000 more than it had dispensed to its customers in 1987. The S.D.D. indicated that the £245,000 was all that it could afford but, in the light of Glenlight's dismay at the inadequacy of the figure, undertook to review the situation at the end of the financial year when the requirements of the other bulk shippers could be more accurately assessed.

It is worth noting that the £245,000 for the customers of Glenlight, the largest bulk shipping operator in the area, was 19% of the total amount available for all bulk shippers. In that year the Scottish Office made £13.6 million available for shipping subsidies which was allocated as follows:

Caledonian-MacBrayne	£6.050m
Orkney/Shetland Services	£6.300m
Bulk Shipments	£1.265m

Eventually it was announced that T.R.S. would become available for timber movements from mainland Highlands to mainland Lowlands which boosted the prospects for both conventional shipping and the tug-and-barge. The possibility of an examination of the whole operation of the T.R.S. by independent external consultants was mooted. These two developments gave Glenlight encouragement for the future. It was genuinely expected that Glenlight's outstanding problems would be resolved in the coming year and that 1994 would see the company on a new footing. This view was mistaken. In fact the puffer trade was not to have a 1994.

The Light Extinguished

As the end of the 1992 fiscal year approached the S.D.D. had, as good as its promise, reviewed its likely spend on T.R.S. and indicated that it expected to be underspent in the bulk shipping allocation and that a retrospective relaxation of some of the restrictions on applying T.R.S. could be considered. Glenlight therefore sought a relaxation of the rules on timber and a direct subvention of the losses on the trading of the experimental timber barge project because of its innovative nature. (The barge trials had cost Glenlight money, even after a grant from H.I.E., as the H.I.D.B. had now become, as the system could not be viable with just the one experimental barge.)

The S.D.D. offer finally took the form of a deficit grant of £200,000 in respect of 1992, which the company thankfully accepted not least for the implication that its problems in trading to the H.I.E. area were being appreciated.

In view of what was to happen at the end of 1993 it is worth recording here the discussions that accompanied this offer. Glenlight had often made the point that it could not indefinitely sustain losses and that it would have to withdraw its ships, however reluctant it would be to cease a valued and long established service. This was no idle threat as its ultimate owners, the shareholders of Clyde Shipping Co., were not in any way bound to provide a 'lifeline service', to use the S.D.D.'s phrase, at private cost. The Scottish Office was understandably concerned that the company would take the money and run and they clearly wanted Glenlight to provide its services in 1993. They therefore sought to bind Glenlight to continue to operate in 1993 if it received the subvention for 1992. Equally understandably the company was not prepared to make an unconditional commitment to trade throughout 1993 irrespective of developing circumstances as, apart from anything else, much would depend on the outcome of the independent inquiry into the operation of the T.R.S. Scheme. Both sides appreciated the other's point of view and finally no promises were asked for or given. The grant was paid and accepted in good faith and Glenlight went into 1993 determined to trade as effectively as it could in the circumstances that would

The less romantic side of the pufferman's life. On Christmas Day 1972, *Raylight* suffered engine failure in a Force 9 gale off Islay. The ship was recovered and went back into service. The crew were rescued by the Islay lifeboat when the ship's anchor started to drag. The temporary lifeboat with open cockpit is seen here standing by. The Coxswain got a bronze medal for the rescue.

The traditional method of transporting timber where there was no pier or jetty was to raft it out to a coaster lying just offshore. The crew of *Elizabeth* of 1866 are getting wet handling this load. Definitely a summer job. (Scottish Maritime Museum)

prevail.

Encouraged by the technical success of the barge trial the timber users began to commit themselves to ordering the annual equivalent of 135,000 tons of logs. This proving of the market encouraged the ordering of a second barge and the chartered 1,200 tonner was bought in and renamed *Glenrosa* to complement and sustain the normal West Coast business. Apart from timber, the company planned to carry in excess of 40,000 tons of coal, salt, fertilisers and building materials. For the 1993/4 fiscal year the S.D.D. increased the discount allocation to £350,000 in recognition of the likely growth in Glenlight's tonnage.

The increase of £100,000 for Glenlight was significant, but it came from an allocation for bulk shippers as a whole that only increased by £20,000, so that it was clear that other shippers were expecting to be less busy. The Orkney/Shetland Service was given an increase of 6% while Cal-Mac's increase of £1.115 million to £7.165 million was equivalent to 18%.

The announcement of the independent enquiry into the operation of the T.R.S. System had been expected in February 1993 so that a report and recommendations would have been available for implementation for the start of the financial year in April 1994. Unease was felt when no announcement had been made by May 1993. The greater the delay the greater would be the uncertainty in Glenlight's planning for 1994. It certainly could not go on sustaining losses while Government took its time deciding on the future of T.R.S.

The announcement, when it came, had

a considerable sting in the tail. The Secretary of State for Scotland linked the review to an investigation into the possible privatisation of Caledonian-MacBrayne. The timetable required the consultants, K.P.M.G., to report on T.R.S. in two stages, by September and by December 1993. The answer to the privatisation question was to be completed in March 1994. The privatisation study, the third Cal-Mac was to be subject to in seven years, set alarm bells ringing in coastal shipping circles. Rightly or wrongly the shipowners believed, from past experience, that while such investigations were going on Government's attitude to them hardened. Decision making processes

Correct stowage of timber is important. *Glenshira* could have been in some difficulties had the weather been less kind but she made a safe passage to Oban where the cargo was re-stowed. (Scottish Maritime Museum)

slowed down because 'The consultant's report is awaited.' At such times of introspection it was tempting for investigators to assume that Cal-Mac could take over the bulk traffic and to ignore the burden that would be thrown onto the roads. (It would probably not even be in their remit to consider this aspect.) After all Cal-Mac was getting over £7 million in 1993 so why could it not do everything for this size of grant? And if Cal-Mac's turnover went up as the coasters disappeared would it not become more attractive to a would-be purchaser?

On previous occasions Glenlight had taken its arguments to the Scottish Office in private and had not always been spectacularly successful in the results it had achieved. There had been times when the judicious application of public pressure had paid dividends. Mrs. MacArthur's coal was a case in point. Professional

public relations consultants, Scottish and Westminster Communications, were appointed to advise on making the public aware of the company's arguments. A three-pronged strategy was adopted; the well rehearsed case would continue to be pressed to the S.D.D., innovative solutions to the T.R.S. problem would be submitted to K.P.M.G., who would be given full co-operation with their investigations and a public 'Save the Puffers' campaign would be started.

The story was taken up well by the Scottish press. The Editorial from *The Herald*, reproduced below, demonstrates the support given and summarises the arguments eloquently. *West Highland Free*

With an article on Glenlight and the 'Bill' cartoon on the front page *The Herald* weighed in with Editorial support on 29th July 1993.

Press adopted a sturdily supportive stance. Some were impressed that *The Times* of London, as distinct from that of Oban, printed an article and a picture. Television played its part in the campaign with a series of interviews with company personnel accompanied by many shots of Hebridean beauty spots, and reference to the various 'Para Handy' programmes. A documentary, made by the independent production company, Fairline Productions, was broadcast by B.B.C. Scotland in early November as part of its *'Focal Point'* series. Glenlight had no editorial influence over the content of the programme which concentrated on the part played by coastal shipping on the economies and the environment of the Hebrides. From the interviews with islanders there emerged a revealing bitterness, born of their distance from the

A sea-borne tradition

THE last of the puffers? Strictly speaking the vessels plying today's offshore trade to the west coast and its islands are not the puffers of Para Handy's time. Their going would, however, bring to an end that sea-borne tradition encapsulated in Neil Munro's tales: they, and their laughter, will live on, but their subject will eventually be fossilised.

Such is a common fate of human enterprise, but in this case the obsequies may be premature. Glenlight Shipping, which is one of the two mainstays of the surviving west coastal network, is not motivated by sentiment but by need and profit. It meets needs which have not entirely disappeared even in the age of the motor car, which realigned West Highland communications from a mainly east-west waterborne axis to a mainly north-south road one. True, aircraft have re-established the old axis, but hardly for bulky items. For these, at least for the islands, the sea must continue to be crossed, and that crossing

has to be subsidised. This is Glenlight's point. It needs the subsidy it receives at present to be augmented and assured over more than a single year. This will seem sound to anyone who runs a business, where a year is too short, and even arbitrary, to be useful: planning capital costs, especially, needs a longer time-scale than 12 months.

Even politicians, often dismissed as short-termists, are known to think in terms of four years — Harold Wilson's famous "quadrennial spasm" informing their forward thinking all the time. In this case, Glenlight's threat to terminate a tradition 150 years old need not be dismissed as an example of "tartan-mail". The small island communities it serves need its attention which means that the Scottish Office should consider its pleas sympathetically along with, and not in competition with, those of Caledonian MacBrayne — that is if it wants small and economically fragile communities to continue to prosper, as it surely must.

"ACH IF DOUGIE WAS HERE HE WOULD TELL THEM HIMSELF"

'Bill' produces a daily topical cartoon for the front page of *The Herald*. This was his response when the news broke in 1993 that Glenlight was likely to go under if a solution was not found to its problems in the West Highland trade. His 'Para Handy' allusions will be instantly recognisable to all who have read Neil Munro's tales.

centre, towards St. Andrews House and its perceived indifference to their situation. The Scottish Office had, under their 'open Government' approach, set up telephone lines to allow the public access on matters of concern to them. They were inundated with calls about Glenlight. There was no doubt about public awareness of what had been previously a private and esoteric debate about shipping subsidies.

A stream of MPs, from all political parties in Scotland, including those from the party of Government, flowed through the company's offices to be briefed on why a capped T.R.S. could not work and what was needed to resolve the problem. They supported Glenlight and applied appropriate Parliamentary pressure by laying down questions in the House and writing directly to Ministers. The Member for Argyll and Bute instigated an adjournment debate. To all, the S.D.D., the consultants and the politicians, the company's stance was the same:

- If the lifeline services were to be maintained they had to subsidised to a level that met all reasonable costs and allowed the participating companies to make a profit, related to the capital employed in providing the service. (The United States Government had recognised this in its relationship with Glenlight.)
- There were strong environmental arguments in favour of retaining the bulk shipping services and keeping heavy traffic off the narrow and difficult to maintain Highland roads. (The tug/barge concept won an environmental award in December 1993 in a competition sponsored by *The Sunday Times* and K.P.M.G.)
- The subsidy regime, in whatever form it was to take, should be stable for a period of three to four years, and not subject to annual negotiation and modi-

fication, so as to allow the commercial companies a reasonable planning timescale.
- If it could not be satisfied that it had the opportunity to have a profitable future on the West Highland services, Glenlight would have no alternative but to withdraw from them as it had lost over £1 million on them in the 1987-92 period since the removal, by the S.D.D., of the deficit funding.

The public's perception of the problems had been raised considerably and the feedback from this campaign was very positive. But it seemed that it was never possible to take steps forward in dealing with Government without having to take at least one step backward. The consultants were not appointed to work on their report until August 1993 which made it impossible for them to adhere to the original timetable. Glenlight was informed that the report would be available, and it would know its fate, in 'Spring, 1994'. This was far too late for the company which would have faced going into another potentially loss-making year with the outcome of the review unknown. In fact the consultants' findings were not even available at the end of 1994 and at the time of writing have still not been made public.

Faced with this situation Glenlight approached the S.D.D. in October for help with a deficit grant for 1993. It had been prepared to give such aid in 1992 and the trading circumstances were no different a year later. The expectations were, of course, that the problem would have been well on the way to being solved during 1993 by the consultant's study. Because no Government policy statement had been made in 1993, Glenlight could not assess its future prospects. A decision to go forward into 1994 could be made more easily if recognition was given to the company for what it had done in 1993, i.e.

demonstrated its commitment to West Highland shipping services. The S.D.D was asked to give a grant of £300,000 for the coasters and to demonstrate its stated belief in the future of timber barging by contributing to the continuing development costs. This side of the business had expanded so much that it was in danger of exhausting the T.R.S. cap before the financial year was over. The T.R.S. cap was raised in December, because other shippers had not used their allocation, but the request for deficit support was refused.

Appropriately enough the adjournment debate had been held on St. Andrew's Day and at that time an ominous hardening of Government's attitude towards Glenlight began to appear. Phrases like 'other services would be available if Glenlight decides to withdraw' and 'the company's services cannot be considered essential' were to be found in the Government's correspondence with the company and with MPs. This was patently a misconception on their part. The Glenlight fleet of 2,200 tons deadweight capacity was deployed 60% of its time in the Highlands and Islands and, unless an equivalent capacity (i.e. 1,300 tons) was available the demand could not be satisfied by other shippers. Four companies were said to be straining at their leashes to take over Glenlight's trade and losses. In aggregate these four did not have 1,300 tons deadweight between them. One of them no longer had any ships at all and had no intention of buying any. This company and two others denied any intention of involving themselves in picking up the pieces, pointing out that their ships did not have the cargo handling equipment. It may well be that the S.D.D believed or hoped that the ro-ro ferries would cope?

On December 15th, Glenlight informed the S.D.D. that it was actively planning to withdraw all its shipping in

Puffer service

Sir, — A report suggested that the puffers could finally disappear from the West Highlands. To save the service, all that is needed apparently is £1 million to tide a company over during difficult times.

There are no doubt some who would regard the disappearance of the puffers as progress, but is this so? To replace one of the puffers would require, for one trip, 22 lorries of 20 tons each, not heavy by the standards of today, but regular convoys of such vehicles would soon seriously damage an already inadequate road system.

Then would come calls for taxpayers' money to be spent to repair the damage and bring the roads up to an adequate standard to bear this traffic. When the total cost was looked at, it would vastly exceed the mere £1 million to maintain the puffer service!

David G Guild
53 GRANGE ROAD, EDINBURGH
29 JULY

All the major Scottish papers took up Glenlight's cause throughout 1993. *The Scotsman*, published in Edinburgh, and perceived by some not to be overly interested in West Coast matters, was as vociferous as any. They printed this letter from an Edinburgh gentleman, who saw clearly what the hidden cost would be of letting the bulk shipping service perish.

January 1994. It asked that the decision not to pay any deficit grant be reconsidered. A request for a meeting with the Minister was refused. A letter dated December 22nd expressed regret that Glenlight was to withdraw and stated that, despite the extent of Glenlight's contribution to services in the Western Isles, Government was not in a position to accept an open ended commitment to provide Glenlight with deficit grant in order to maintain its services. (An open ended commitment had not been sought, merely financial support, to tide the company over until the consultants reported.) The writer expressed the hope that his letter had been 'helpful.'

It certainly was not. The year of 1993 had passed and during it the Scottish Office had not produced solutions to well understood problems. It was the year in which Government had suggested that the company had an obligation to keep on trading having accepted retrospective deficit support for 1992. If the support was available in 1992 why was it not available for 1993? The Government's volte-face was never explained. The refusal to meet the 1993 losses even partially, could have been tholed if the uncertainties surrounding the T.R.S. allocations for the next fifteen months had been resolved. These imponderables and the lack of any indications as to what the promised new system might offer coastal shippers in 1995 and beyond, made the decision to withdraw inevitable. The Clyde Shipping shareholders could not continue to lose money supplying services if there were no prospects of the situation improving. The ships were laid up for their Christmas holi-days and did not recommence on the West Highland trade in the new year. Contractual commitments for south-bound timber were met by operating one ship and the barges during 1994. No more northbound cargoes were carried to the Highlands and Islands. In effect the puffer trade was dead.

The 'helpful letter' had been received on Christmas Eve. Media speculation about the future of Glenlight was intense over the holiday period. A formal announcement of the withdrawal of services was made on 6th January 1994. Even as late as this, the Member for Greenock and Port Glasgow, in whose constituency the Glenlight office lay, and the Shadow Minister for Transport tried to persuade the Minister to relent. He did not.

Hay and Hamilton had bowed out in 1976 and now it was the turn of the descendants of Ross and Marshall to leave the stage. For over 130 years the vital links with the West had been preserved by their ships and whatever else may be said of them they could not be faulted for their resource and commitment, particularly in that final decade.

5

EPILOGUE

Within a few short weeks of Glenlight withdrawing its coasters from the Northbound movement of cargoes foreign vessels were landing foreign salt and foreign coal in northern ports on the Scottish mainland and islands. The bulk shipments were broken into 20 ton parcels for road haulage which thundered through towns and villages on the Highlands' fragile road infrastructure. Let us count the cost of the road repair bills before we claim, as some did with undue haste to support their public stances, that lorries were cheaper and better. To reach many of the cargo destinations the heavy vehicles had to take advantage of the nations much subsidised car ferry system which received at that time an operating subsidy of £7 million per annum from the Scottish taxpayer. In the year after Glenlight's closure the number of commercial vehicle using Cal-Mac increased by four thousand. Was this a co-incidence?

It is a bargain is it not for only £7 million? On a day to day basis most would accept that Caledonian MacBrayne operates well. But it does so within a limited strategy. Those few questions that have been asked about the transport infrastructure of the nation's most fragile economic area, the West Highlands and Islands, have been answered by building more and more and bigger and bigger roll-on roll-off ferries. What has been overlooked in all of the few public debates that have taken place is that Cal-Mac offers an East to West solution to what is a South to North problem. Countless vehicle miles have to be travelled on some of the nation's most remote and difficult to maintain roads or Cal-Mac could not function at all. The real and major cost to the islander is in the roads and road vehicles that get essential cargoes to and from the publicly maintained ferry terminals. The millions of pounds of subsidy for ferry operating costs is only the tip of the cost iceberg with which island economies collide.

Academic studies tell us that we underestimate the full social cost of the motor vehicle because we ignore the price of air and noise pollution, accidents and congestion. It has been suggested that motor vehicle taxation should be increased by a factor of five to meet the true cost. Under charging the internal combustion engine, on which the ro-ro ferry is dependent, undermines the viability of more environmentally friendly forms of transport, such as coastal shipping. With coastal shipping a South to North solution is supplied for the South to North transport problem. Instead of seeking a purely cost effective transport system for the West Highlands we impose on it, through its dependency on the car ferry, a costly system which has no possibility of becoming less costly. Hydrocarbon fuel taxes are here to stay and show no signs of decreasing. Further governmental thinking favours toll bridges and road pricing schemes. Ultimately these systems could become a restriction on the use the road network as only those best able to afford the tolls, into which category the Islander does not come, will be able to use them. (It will be interesting to follow the future pattern of toll charges on the new bridge to Skye.) Invest in your vehicle, pay the road tax, buy the fuel for it, hand over the road toll, contribute taxes to operating the ferry and its terminal and pay the tariff to cross the Minches and it will all add up to a tidy sum to get to Uist.

Not all nations are so blinkered. The Swiss intend that within a decade all lorries will be carried across their country by train. The Dutch are capitalising on their magnificent system of inland waterways. In Germany there is a ban on all lorry movements at weekends and they are exercising positive discrimination in favour of the Rhine and canals. The Italians actually operated a sea-borne container service that ran along the coast within sight of the autostrada whose congestion and costs it was intended to alleviate. In Scotland we thrust the South/North burden of transport to our Western seaboard onto narrow and even single track roads for the sake of the apparently cheap East/West sea route.

There is an alternative. It is a coastal bulk and container service for the long North/South axis. Take goods from the central belt off the roads and put them on specialised multi-purpose ships (look to Scandinavia for examples) on inter-island services from the Clyde. Coastal shipping is environmentally friendly and cost effective while the ferry/road mode is neither. Ferries will still be needed but let each type of shipping do what it does best. i. e. does economically. In the past, subsidy fought subsidy and five coaster companies shared £1.3 million and attempted to compete with the ferry's £7 million. Not surprisingly they lost. The £1.3 million is no longer paid out and to that extent has been saved. It would not be difficult to spend more than £1.3 million extra repairing Highland roads.

Thirty years ago, when considering the options for Islay/Jura transport services, the S.D.D. favoured the longer sea routes in preference to an overland route on Jura, balked at the cost of the complete reconstruction of the Jura roads that would have been necessary! Changed times!

The coastal shipping owners were on record for more than a decade advocating the development of an integrated bulk and ferry transport system for the area. (The part to be played by road and rail cannot be ignored in the planning process.) The Norwegian model for planning an integrated transport system for its own West Coast, an area geographically similar to that of Scotland, is worth studying. It depends on stringent control by local and central government with private companies fulfilling an agreed role. Value for money for the Scottish taxpayer (and the Islander is a taxpayer too) and effective support for the fragile economies of the Islands and Highlands have to be the objectives.

So is the puffer really dead? The ships and the people who knew the trade are now widely dispersed. But is the concept still valid? The islands are still there and they have got to be supplied with the basics of life. A purpose-built vessel still offers the same advantages it did a century ago before we became bemused by the motor car. The seed lies dormant, but it will spring to life if nurtured. Perhaps the light is only temporarily dimmed.

Appendix I

LIGHTER OWNERS

The following list is compiled from the author's researches and while it is considered to be comprehensive it is unlikely to be complete in that it does not claim to record every company or skipper/owner who ever traded a lighter in Scotland. It is likely to be more complete for the registered companies like Ross & Marshall, than for the many owners of single ships who traded in local niche markets.

1. Carron Company Ltd. Used numbers as names (Built 12). East & West coast trade in raw materials and finished goods.
2. Leith, Hull and Hamburg Steam Packet Company Ltd. Owned by Jas. Currie. Transhipments mainly from the Forth to Port Dundas. Used letters of the alphabet for names e. g. "A" built 1873 and "Z" built 1889.
3. Morris Munro & Company Ltd. Coal merchants to MacBrayne steamers. Owned *Sylph* and *Faun*.
4. John G. Frew. Owned *Fairlie Glen* and *Ashdale Glen*.
5. W. H. King. Owned *Macbeth* and *Macduff*.
6. Glasgow Steam Coasters Ltd. Managed by Paton and Hendry. Used names such as *Seal* and *Walrus*.
7. T. P. Purdie.
8. Warnock Bros. Ltd. Owned *Douglas*, *Logan*, *Faithful* etc.
9. Shirra Steam Ship Company Ltd. (Colin McPhail & Co. Ltd.)
10. G. & G. Hamilton (Brodick) Ltd.
11. Mackie Brothers (White Horse Distillery -- Scottish Malt Distillers Ltd.). Owned *Pibroch*.
12. George Halliday of Rothesay. Timber merchant. Owned *Elizabeth* and *Craigielea*.
13. Walter Kerr (Millport). Owned *Saxon*.
14. Burrell & Sons. Owned *Goliath*.
15. Jack Brothers Ltd., Greenock. Owned *Challenger*, *Jackite*.
16. Ross and Marshall Ltd. (The Light Shipping Co. Ltd.)
17. J. & J. Hay Ltd. of Kirkintilloch. (Also Cowal Coal & Trading Company Ltd.).
18. Coasting Steamships Ltd. Owned *Innisgara* and other motorised puffers.
19. Colthorpe and Dewar
20. J. Gardner & Sons, Kirkintilloch.
21. J. Ross & Co., Falkirk.
22. Anglo American Oil Co. Ltd. Owned *Perfection*.
23. J. Stewart, Arran, owned *Ashdale Glen*.
24. Steel & Bennie Ltd., owned *Lintie*.
25. J. Glover, Paisley, owned *Craigielee*.
26. G. Halliday, Bute, Owned *Elizabeth* and *Grilse*.
27. J. K. Campbell Ltd, Irvine, owned *Jennie*.
28. Dickson & Company Ltd.
29. Malcolm Campbell & Sons.
30. A. McNeill & Company Ltd., Greenock.
31. M.M. Brown & Company of Greenock. Owned *Glenholm*.

32. F. Dewar of Rothesay.
33. J. Campbell Ltd. (Mac Shipping Company) of Glasgow.
34. Arran Transport & Trading Company. Owned *Arran Rose* and *Arran Monarch*.
35. D. McCorquodale. Owned *Lady Isle*, *Lady Morven*.
36. W. McMillan of Campbeltown. Owned *Halcyon*.
37. Wm. Burke Ltd. of Greenock.
38. H. Carmichael of Craignure. Owned *Marsa*, *Eldessa*.
39. A. F. Henry and J. McGregor Ltd. of Leith.
40. Wm. Robertson Ltd. Owned *Jasper* and *Diamond*.
41. Alexander Baillie (Troon). Owned *Hafton, Advance* and *Elim*.
42. Alister Kelso (Arran).
43. J. McCreath (Hunter's Quay).
44. Aitken & Company (Falkirk).
45. John Kelly & Company Ltd. (Belfast).
46. Dougall & Stirrat.
47. A. Leslie (Glasgow).
48. Greenhill and Craig (Belfast).
49. C. & J. Lamont of Tiree.
50. Irvine Shipping & Trading Company Ltd.
51. Easdale Shipping Ltd.
52. Glenlight Shipping Ltd.

These four probably began life as horse-drawn mineral barges on the Forth or Monkland canals. The name *Gartsherrie* certainly suggest affinity with Baird's Ironworks on the Monkland. The absence of either a mast and derrick for cargo handling or bulwarks to keep water off the deck is proof that they were not intended to operate anywhere but in calm waters. The large vessel on the inside berth has a steering wheel suggesting that she is the youngest of the group.

Appendix II

LIGHTER BUILDERS

It is not claimed that the list below is definitive but it is representative of the major builders whose lighters traded on the Scottish canals and coasts. The Hamiltons, who built only one ship, the first and wooden hulled, *Glencloy* would not qualify as shipbuilders in this context. There were six other English East Coast yards which built VICS in World War II but only those listed below had their product bought subsequently by Scottish owners and traded in Scotland.

1. Burrell Shipyards, Hamiltonhill and Dumbarton.
2. McNicoll Bros., Maryhill.
3. Scott & Sons Ltd., Bowling.
4. P. McGregor and Company Ltd., Kirkintilloch.
5. J. & J. Hay Ltd., Kirkintilloch.
6. Crawford & Company, Kirtintilloch.
7. Swan & Co., Maryhill.
8. Cumming & Swan, Blackhill.
9. Larne Shipbuilding Company Ltd.
10. Ross and Marshall Ltd., Greenock.
11. D. R. Dunston Ltd, Thorne. (VICs).
12. I. Pimbolt and Sons Ltd., Northwich. (VICs).
13. G. Goole Shipbuilding and Repair Company Ltd., Goole. (VICs).
14. B. Brown Shipbuilding Company Ltd., Hull. (VICs).
15. Fleming & Ferguson Ltd., Paisley.
16. Livingston & Company Ltd., Peterhead.
17. Wm Jackson & Co., Port Dundas.
18. Marshall & Co., Kelvindock.
19. Ferguson & Co., Firhill.
20. Ferguson Bros.(Port Glasgow) Ltd.
21. W. Denny & Bros Ltd., Dumbarton.
22. Grangemouth Dockyard Co. Ltd.
23. Scottish Iron Co., Irvine.
24. J. Harker Ltd., Knottingley. (VICs).
25. James Pollock & Sons Co. Ltd., Faversham. (VICs).
26. W. J. Yarwood & Sons Ltd., Northwich.

Appendix III

J. HAY AND SONS LTD.
Operating Results: 1938

Tabulated below are the income and cost figures for nine* of Hay's lighters for 1938. The ships in question were all coasting or outside boats. They were capable of canal work but had raised bulwarks, hatch coamings and covers to meet Government regulations for ships going outside the smooth water limits of the Clyde Estuary. They had a crew of four.

	£ 000	
Income	21.32	
Costs :		% of Costs
Insurance	0.62	3.70
Repairs etc	1.83	11.00
Port charges	3.94	23.80
Canal charges	0.80	4.80
Crew wages	6.25	37.70
Coal	3.14	19.00
	16.58	100.00
'Profit'	4.74	

The average profit per ship was just over £520 for the year. Note that no depreciation had been charged in this method of reporting. Hence the italicising of the word 'Profit'. A deduction for depreciation is essential to arrive at the true contribution made toward the overhead costs of the business.

During the year the ships burnt 2,822 tons of coal at an average cost of £1.11/ton. Fuel and crew wages were the two most expensive items accounting for almost 60% of costs. Lighter operating was to remain highly sensitive to these two costs throughout the remainder of the steam era.

During this year the whole Hay fleet of twenty-two, which included thirteen inside boats, carried a total of 210,000 tons of cargo, 44,000 tons of which was canal traffic. Almost 90% of the canal tonnage was timber battens.

* The vessels operating were *Tartar, Druid, Kype, Moor, Spartan, Serb, Tuscan, Anzac* and *Lascar*.

Appendix IV

ROSS AND MARSHALL LTD.
Profit/Loss Account For 1882

	£	s	d				
Net profit from ships	1,991	4.	11	Expenses	(483	12.	9)
Net profit from steam				Interest on overdraft	(310	14	8)
winches	220	13	3	Bad debt	(78	15	7)
Profit from cartage	88	14	6				
Profit from workshop	70	1	7	Profit 3800		16	11
Profit from salvage	643	19	11				
Profit from coal sales	705	4	10				
Profit from stevedoring	984	0	11				

Clearly from the above, shipping was the most important profit making activity, twice the level of stevedoring, the next highest contributor.

Appendix V

ROSS AND MARSHALL LTD.
Profit/loss account for ss *Daylight*, 1879

The ledger shows the following for the steam lighter *Daylight*:

	£	s	d
Freights earned	988	19	4
Expenses	325	8	2
Interest to A. Ross	217	9	5
Interest to J. Marshall	217	9	5
To P/L Account	228	12	4
Balance	0	0	0

This balance was drawn up in the pre-depreciation days of accounting. *Daylight* was valued at £1,300 in 1874 and on the basis of a twenty year life £65 per annum should otherwise have been deducted for depreciation before declaring a profit. This was the practice in Ross and Marshall after 1900. Regrettably, no detail of the expenses is available and it seems remarkable that on a turnover of £989 a gross profit of £663, 67%, was made. This is much higher than the Hays made on the *Lyra*. (See page 40)

Appendix VI
SHIPS' LOGS 1880–1963

ss *Starlight*, (March, 1880)

1st–2nd	At Greenock awaiting orders
3rd	Furniture from Greenock to Kilcreggan
4th	Coal from Glasgow to Ayr
5th	Greenock loading coal for Girvan
6th	On passage to Girvan
7th	At Girvan (Sunday)
8th–10th	At Girvan discharging
11th	On passage to Port Dundas
12th–14th	Port Dundas awaiting orders
15th	Loading coal for Innellan
16th	On passage Innellan
17th	At Innellan discharging
18th	On passage to Glasgow
19th	At Glasgow loading coal for Girvan
20th	On passage Girvan
21st	At Girvan (Sunday)
22nd–23rd	Discharging at Girvan
24th	On passage to Glasgow
25th	At Glasgow loading a boiler for Greenock
26th	Discharging at Greenock
27th	Loading coal at Glasgow for Hunters Quay
28th	At Sandbank (Sunday)
29th	Discharging at Hunters Quay
30th	On passage to Glasgow
31st	Loading coal at Glasgow

Number of Days working	24 (77%)
Number of Days idle	3 (10%)
"Lost" Sundays	4 (12%)

ss*Starlight*, (March, 1963)

1st–4th	At Greenock awaiting order (including Sunday)
5th	On passage to Furnace
6th	Loading stone for Glasgow
7th	On passage to Glasgow
8th	Discharging Glasgow
9th	On hire to Cunard
10th	On passage to Troon (Sunday)
11th	Troon loading coal for Dunoon
12th–13th	Dunoon discharging
14th	Troon loading coal for Rothesay
15th	Troon weatherbound
16th	On passage to Rothesay, discharge started
17th	At Rothesay (Sunday)
18th	Rothesay discharging
19th	Troon loading coal for Tarbert, Loch Fyne.
20th–21st	Tarbert discharging
22nd	Troon loading coal for Dunoon
23rd	At Dunoon discharging
24th	At Greenock (Sunday)
25th	At Greenock awaiting on hir
26th	On hire J& J Denholm
27th	On hire United States Navy
28th	At Greenock awaiting orders
29th–30th	On hire MV *Betelgeuse*
31st	On hire Cunard.

Number of Days working	22 (71%)
Number of Days idle	5 (16%)
Number of Days weatherbound	1 (3%)
"Lost" Sundays	3 (10%)

MV *Raylight*, (October 1963)

1st	At Rothesay discharging
2nd	At Greenock awaiting orders
3rd	Greenock loading explosives for Carrickfergus
4th	Carrickfergus discharging
5th	At Ardrossan loading barley for Port Ellen
6th	On passage to Port Ellen (Sunday)
7th–8th	Discharging at Port Ellen
9th	On passage to Ardrossan
10th	At Ardrossan loading barley for Port Ellen
11th–12th	Port Ellen discharging
13th	At Campbeltown (Sunday)
14th	At Campbeltown loading stone for Gigha
15th–16th	At Gigha discharging
17th	At Belfast loading scrap for Glasgow
18th	Glasgow discharging
19th	At Greenock awaiting orders
20th	At Greenock (Sunday)
21st	On passage to Troon
22nd	Troon loading road metal for Port Ellen
23rd	On passage to Port Ellen, weatherbound at Campbeltown
24th–25th	Port Ellen discharging
26th	On passage to Ardrossan
27th	At Ardrossan (Sunday)
28th	At Ardrossan loading malt for Bruichladdich
29th	Bruichladdich discharging
30th	Bruichladdich loading whisky for Glasgow
31st	On passage to Glasgow

Number of Days working	26 (85%)
Number of Days idle	2 (6%)
Number of Days weatherbound	1 (3%)
"Lost" Sundays	2 (6%)

Appendix VII

STOWAGE MEASUREMENTS

The following list indicates the considerable range of cargo types that were carried in the coasters and is reproduced from a 1940s notebook. Not all of these exotic cargoes were carried to the Western Isles. Many would be the basis of lighterage work in the canals and transhipments in the Firth of Clyde.

Such tables would be the basis for calculating freight rates for quoting to customers. Thus a ship with a hold capacity of 7,000 cubic feet, such as a typical 88 foot Crinan Canal boat, would be expected to take around 140 tons of coal at 49 cubic feet per ton. A daily income rate, times the number of days estimated to load, deliver and discharge the cargo, divided by the 140 tons would indicate the freight/ton required. On the other hand coke at 90 cubic feet per ton would fill the hold with about 80 tons, without sinking the vessel to her marks, and require a much higher freight rate per ton (nearly double) to make a profit. Pig iron would load the ship to her Plimsoll line with her hold barely a quarter full.

In the 1930s when the Hay boats were carrying 50,000 tons per annum on the Forth and Clyde Canal, 75% of this total was timber battens.

Jarrah is an Australian hardwood which was used for heavy duty purposes e.g. railway sleepers.

	Cubic feet per ton
Asphalt in barrels or drums	48
Bricks, in bulk	21
(fire) in bulk	28
Cement in bags	34
China clay in bags	42
in bulk	40
Coal	42/49
Coke, foundry	80
gas	90
Copra, in bales	95
Cork, pressed bales	200
Cotton, Am. high density pressed	115
Egyptian, bales	70
Indian, bales	55
Esparato Grass in bales	140

FRUIT:
Bananas in crates	110
Currants in boxes	50
Figs in boxes	50
Lemons in boxes	85
Grapes in casks	90
Melons in boxes	80
Onions in boxes	80
Oranges in boxes	85
Prunes in boxes	52
Raisins in boxes	50
Fuel, oil in bulk	40

GRAIN:
Barley in bulk	54
in bags	60
Maize in bulk	48
in bags	55
Oats in bulk	65/70
in bags	70/75
Rye in bags	55
in bulk	50

Wheat in bulk	48	Grass	50
in bags	50	Hemp	70
Hemp in bales	90	Linseed	60
Iron, pig	12	Mustard	62
Lead, pig	9	Poppy	70
Locust beans in bulk	85	Rape	60
Molasses, in casks	60	Sunflower	110
in bulk	28	Soya Beans	58
Nuts, ground nuts, bulk	110	Sugar in bags	48
Oilcake	50	Tar, in barrels	55
Ore, iron	18/25		
Phosphate, in bulk	28/35	TIMBER	
Pit props	60	Deals, boards and battens	
Pitch, in barrels	45	1 standard weighs about	70/90
Potatoes, in barrels	80	3 tons and stows in 265'	
in bags	70	Jarrah	
Rice, in bags	50	1 standard 5.25 tons	30
Salt, in bulk	35	1 load of 50 cu. ft.	32
in bags	38	Pitchpine	
Sand, in bulk	22	1 standard 3.5/4ft.	70
		Tin, Ingots	10
SEEDS, in bags		Wool, varies greatly	100/240
Canary	60	Water, fresh	36
Cloves	50	Salt	35

Appendix VIII

LIGHTER OWNERSHIP
1939–1966

OWNERS	No. Of Ships	1939 Dates Of Building	Deadweight (Tons)	No. Of Ships	1966 Dates Of Building	Deadweight (Tons)
J.Hay & Sons Ltd.	20	1896–1939	2330	9*	1941–1966	1515
Ross & Marshall	8	1885–1938	900	7	1916–1965	1525
Warnock Bros. Ltd.	5	1882–1926	590			
G.& G. Hamilton Ltd.	3	1910–1935	425	*		
C. McPhail & Co. Ltd.	3	1903–1905	405	**		
J.K. Campbell Ltd.	3	1895–1910	355	2***	1941–1946	260
A. McNeil Ltd.	3	1901–1907	355			
R. Cameron & Co. Ltd.	2	1908–1909	275			
G.M. Paterson Ltd.	2	1905–1921	275			
Other Owners	10	1878–1920	985	4	1941–1946	520
Total	59		6860	22		3820

NO. OF SHIPS			
70 to 110 tons dwt.	24		0
120 to 140 tons dwt.	27		12
140 to 165 tons dwt.	8		5
240 to 290 tons dwt.	0		5
Total	59		22

* Amalgamated to form Hay-Hamilton in 1963
** Amalgamated with G.&G. Hamilton in 1948
*** 50% owned by Ross & Marshall, as Irvine Shipping & Trading Ltd.

Note that the number of ships in 1966 has fallen to 37% of the 1939 level while the deadweight tonnage has fallen only to 56% of the 1939 capacity.

Note also that in 1939 the ships of the smaller owners are quite old, mostly built pre-1910. By 1966 these owners are no longer in business.

Appendix IX

COMPANY LIVERIES

Ross and Marshall
Hull: Black
Funnel: Red with a black top separated
          by a broad white band above a
          narrow black band.

G. & G. Hamilton
Hull: Black
Funnel: Red with a black top.

J. and J. Hay
Hull: Black.
Funnel: Pink with a black top.

Irvine Shipping and Trading
Hull: Black.
Funnel: Black with red top.

Glenlight Shipping (1974)
Hull: Black (later red)
Funnel: Red with black top and a black
          "G" inside a white circle.

Appendix X

Why T.R.S. Did and Did Not Work

Tariff Rebate Subsidy was paid to the cargo receiver as a discount on the freight charged by the shipping company, thus:

Freight charged by Glenlight per ton	£10.00
T.R.S. @ 30%	(3.00)
Amount paid by cargo receiver to Glenlight	£7.00

But if Glenlight was not making a profit at £10 and actually needed to charge £12 then the calculation became:

Freight charged by Glenlight per ton	£12.00
T.R.S. @ 30%	(3.60)
Amount paid by cargo receiver to Glenlight	£ 8.40

and so the Islander paid £1.40 or 20% more.

However, if the T.R.S. rate was increased to just over 40% then the Islander still paid £7.00, thus:

Freight charged by Glenlight per ton	£12.00
T.R.S. @ 42%	£(5.00)
Amount paid by cargo receiver to Glenlight	£7.00

In the early days of T.R.S. application the S.D.D. in effect paid Glenlight the difference between the £10 and the £12 freight with the deficit subsidy. When it withdrew the deficit payment in 1987 and did not put up the T.R.S. rate Glenlight's H.I.D.B. trading went into the red.

It also becomes apparent that if the T.R.S. allocation is restricted, or capped, at £245,000 p.a. then it can only be offered for 82,000 tons of commodities if the average T.R.S. discount is £3.00/ton. (£245,000 ÷ £3 = 82,000). If however the average T.R.S. per ton is £3.60 then it can only be offered on 68,000 tons if the cap is kept at £245,000 per annum. This was the Catch 22 situation with capping: if you put your freights up you could not carry enough tonnage to be profitable as the T.R.S. allocation got used up too quickly. If you did not put your rates up then you could carry more tons before the allocation was spent but you carried all of those tons at a loss.

Little wonder then that Glenlight was constantly asking to have the workings of the T.R.S. system reviewed.

Appendix XI

Effect of Government Subsidy on (Loss) in H.I.D.B. Area Trading, 1979–1987
Glenlight Shipping Ltd.

H.I.D.B Area Profit/Loss (£'000)

	1979	1980	1981	1982	1983	1984	1985	1986	1987
Loss	(92.6)	(128.3)	(24.7)	(116.7)	(103.1)	(84.1)	(118.3)	(77.1)	(107.2)
Deficit Grant	Nil	100	70	112.1	111.5	129.5	120	91.1	45
Total	(92.6)	(28.3)	42.6	(4.5)	8.4	45.4	1.7	14	(62.2)

Overall Company Profit/(Loss) (£'000)

	1979	1980	1981	1982	1983	1984	1985	1986	1987
H.I.D.B.	(92.6)	(28.3)	42.6	(4.5)	8.4	45.4	1.7	14	(62.2)
Others	80.3	16.9	(8.4)	86.8	93.3	91.4	122.4	124.7	(72.8)
Total	(12.3)	(11.4)	34.2	82.3	101.7	136.8	124.1	138.7	(135.0)

Total Cost To Government Of Subsidising H.I.D.B. Freights (£'000)

	1979	1980	1981	1982	1983	1984	1985	1986	1987
Deficit Grant	Nil	100	70	112.1	111.5	129.5	120	91.1	45
T.R.S On Freight	Nil	112	130	157	158.3	156.6	144.9	191.8	239.6
Total	Nil	212	200	269.1	269.8	286	264.9	282.9	284.6

Appendix XII

COMMODITIES CARRIED ANNUALLY ('000) TONS) 1973–1993

by Glenlight Shipping Ltd.

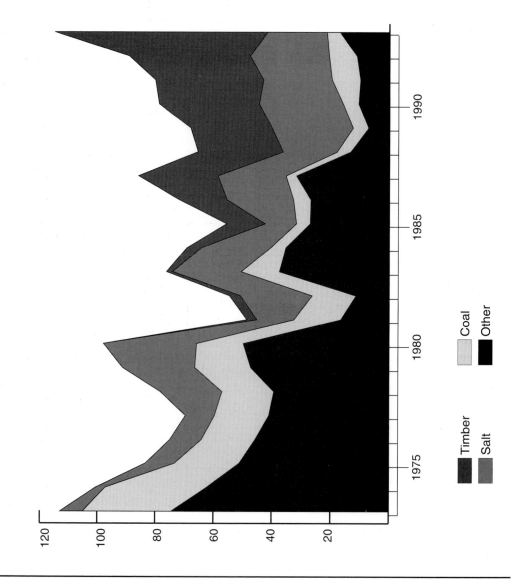

Appendix XIII

TONNAGES DELIVERED TO HIGHLANDS IN 1987

by Glenlight Shipping Ltd.

LOCATION	COAL	BLOCKS	STONE	SALT	MISC	TOTAL
Dunoon				800		800
Bute				240		240
Gigha			4459			4459
Islay	126			250		376
Jura	76					76
Tiree	753				1275	2028
Coll	132					132
Colonsay	78		359			437
Mull			975	450		1425
Lismore	174					174
Skye	94	190		3700	420	4404
Rhum	88				57	145
Canna	30				136	166
Vatersay	45					45
Berneray	177					177
Eriskay	91					91
Scalpay	443					43
Raasay				100		100
Barra	383					383
Lochboisedale	128	335				463
Lochmaddy	120	858				705
Loch Carnan		6060	361	1400		7821
Leverborough			1050			1050
Tarbert (Harris)	99			700		799
Keose				1050		1050
Stornoway	583			700	3295	4578
Iona		350	700		130	1180
Campbeltown			357	250		607
Tarbert (L. Fyne)				100		100
Ardrishaig				1650		1650
Portavadie			3370			3370
Oban				2055		2055
Corpach				4720		4720
Kyle of Lochalsh				1030		1030
Gairloch					650	650
Kinlochbervie				1400		1400
Lochinver				1050		1050
TOTAL	3260	7520	10581	23255	5313	50289

In addition 27,274 tons of logs were carried south

Appendix XIV

THE DEVELOPMENT OF THE TUG AND BARGE CONCEPT FOR THE SHIPMENT OF TIMBER

The development of the tug/barge concept for timber came from the increased demand for West Highland timber in the late 1980s and early 1990s. Glenlight was moving around 35,000 tons of logs annually by 1990 using its coasters. The projections were that this was to increase to 100,000 tons by 1995 and to 300,000 by the end of the century if, as was expected, paper making capacity in Scotland was doubled. In considering how to cope with such an increase, Glenlight very quickly came to the conclusion that its conventional Highland shipping technique was not the answer. The area had few suitable ports and none close to the ten possible loading sites, adjacent to the mature forests, which had been identified as source points.

For various technical reasons parcels were likely to be in the range of 400 to 600 tons and it was desirable to load the ship as close to the forest as possible. When using coasters, timber was felled, loaded onto road transport and then stacked on a pier. When enough had been stored to fill a full ship's hold, a coaster was put alongside to load herself from the jetty with her crane. The process was slow, involved double-handling and was restricted to locations, becoming ever more rare in the West Highlands, where there was a quay with adequate storage space. (With the advent of the Ro-Ro ferry, which needed loading ramps, many traditional piers had

been modified or had fallen into disrepair.)

The proposed solution was a tug and barge system. The barge would be beached on the forests' shores, using techniques that were second-nature to a puffer company, and the timber would be loaded directly from the road transport without double-handling. Tugs would be supplied by Glenlight's sister company in the Clyde Shipping Group, Clyde Shipping Tugs. Puffer know-how would be married to equally venerable towage savvy to solve the problem. The concept envisaged one tug servicing three 600 ton deadweight barges on the basis of having one barge loading, one on passage and one discharging. In this way, one motive unit would be economically provided for three cargo carrying units. The expensive part of the system, the tug, was not kept idle while the relatively slow processes of loading and discharging went on. It was not planned that the barges should completely replace the conventional ship. The two systems would complement each other and share the load as the tonnages increased and the barges went through their proving trials.

The barges offered the possibility of keeping the potentially huge increase in log transport (to around 300,000 tons per annum) away from long road haulage with distinct environmental advantages for the Highlands where road infrastructure was fragile. The 1988 review of the T.R.S. system put severe restrictions on the application of discounts for timber cargoes. It was argued by Glenlight that if the environmentally kind tug/barge method was to be kick-started then freight discounts, in the form already applied to conventional shipping, should be made available. After persuasion by both Glenlight and the Forestry Commission, based on the economic and environmental advantages of timber barging, the S.D.D. relaxed the restrictions and became supportive. Two barges were built, one in 1992 and another in 1993, and demonstrated the viability of the approach.(The large increase in the timber tonnage carried by Glenlight in 1993 was due to barging.) It was never fully tested with three barges as T.R.S. was withdrawn in 1995 and the experiment was discontinued.

INDEX OF SHIPS' NAMES

Illustrations in the text are denoted in *italic*; colour plate numbers are in **bold**

A, 9, 111
Aaron Manby, 12
Acolyte, 48
Advance, 112
Ardfern, *25*, 76, *77*
Alecto, 12
Anzac, 28, 74, 114
Archimedes, 12
Arran Rose, 112
Arran Monarch, 112
Arclight, *50*, 51
Ashdale Glen, 111
Boer, 47, 74,
Briton, 23, 39
Challenger, 111
Charlotte Dundas, *11*, 12, 17, 19
Chindit, 39, 74
Celt, 39, 66, 74
Chrysolite, 48
Clydeforth, 67
Comet, 17,
Craigielea, 111
Cretan, **1**, 62, 74,
Cuban, 74,
Cupid, 17
Dane, 74
Dawnlight, **6**, 31, 32, *32*, *33*, 36, 55, 56
Daylight, 114
Delta, *37*
Diamond, 112
Douglas, 111
Druid, 44, *46*, 74, 82, *83*, 114
Eldessa, 112
Electriclight, 48
Elim, 112
Elizabeth, *102*, 111
Evandale, 66
Fairlie Glen, 111
Faithful, 47, 111
Faun, 111
Flying Spray, **1**
Gael, 22, 74,
Gartsherrie, *112*
Glasgow, 13, 20, 37
Glenaray, 44, *70*
Gleannshira, 42

Glencloy, 25, 28, 32, 36, 39, 41, *41*, 42, *44*, 46, *59*, 82, *83*, 87, 88, 95, *96*
Glenetive, 36, 86, *87*, 88
Glenfyne, **3**, **5**, 25, *31*, 32, 36, 45, 46, 99
Glenholm, 111
Glenrosa, 36, 88, 102
Glensheil, 19, 32, 33, 36, *56*, 85, *90*
Glenshira, 29, *29*, 30, *30*, 31, 44, *73*, 82, *103*
Goliath, 111
Great Britain, 12
Greek, 38, 74
Grilse, 111
Hafton, 112
Halcyon, 112
Hecla, HMS, *45*
Hero, *67*
Inca, 47, 74,
Innisbeg, 26, 27
Innisgara, 26, *26*, 111
Invercloy, **4**, *25*, 29, 41, 42
Isle of Gigha, 78
Jackite, 111
Jasper, 112
Jennie, 111
Kaffir, 28, *30*, 74, 85
Kelpie, 21, *23*, 24
Kype, 114
Lascar, 28, 74, 82, 114
Lady Isle, 112
Lady Morven, 112
Leopold, 22
Linnet, 14, *15*
Lintie, 111
Logan, 111
Lyra, 38, *40*, 41, 114
Macbeth, 111
Macduff, 111
Marsa, 112
Moonlight, 48, 53, 54, *54*, 67, *80*
Moor, 74, 114
Nos. 10, 11 &12, 10
Nelson, 39, *40*, 41
Norman, 39

Otter, *24*
Perfection, *45*, 111
Pibroch, *15*, *17*, 30, *69*, 77, 111
Polarlight, *9*, 36, *55*, 69, 82, 88, 98
Politician, 47
Princess Mayse, *18*, 19
Pyroscaphe, 12
Queensgate, 55
Rattler, 12
Raylight, 51, 55, 56, *57*, 71, 72, *101*, 117
Rivercloy, 41, *59*, 63, *64*, 76
Roman, 38, 58, *58*
Saxon, 38, 39, 111
Seal, 111
Sealight, 28, 36, *52*, 88, 100
Searchlight, 48
Serb, **1**, **2**, 74, 114
Smeaton, *12*,
Sound of Gigha, 81
Sound of Islay, 81
Sir James, *27*
Slav, 74, *75*
Spartan, 28, *64*, 66, 74, *84*, *85*, 114
Sprucelight, **8**, 127
Starlight, 48, 67, 71, 72, 117
Stormlight, 30, 36, *53*, 54, 56, 67, 82, *83*, 85
Sunlight, 22
Sylph, 111
Tartar, 114
Texan, 74,
Tiree, *66*
Thomas, 13, *14*, 19, 20, 37, 38
Tom Moore, *21*, 23
Trial, 12
Trojan, 74
Turk, *39*, 74, *75*
Tuscan, 29, 66, 74, 114
Victor, *66*
Vulcan, 12, *13*, 17,
Walrus, 111
Warlight, 25, 48, 82
Wib, *86*
Z, 9, 111
Zephon, *63*